Contents

CD Rom

The first section of the CD Rom contains practical guidance on some of the key points from the book. These will be found via a number of practical activities based on specific chapters of the book. Although most of the activities are based on specific chapters, some of the more general strategies are based on the book as a whole.

Wherever the CD Rom icon appears, the reader should go to the CD Rom for an electronic version of the material.

The second part of the CD Rom is a PowerPoint presentation based on the book and can be contextualised for staff development activities.

Section 1

Activities

Activity 1	Developing independence in learning (based on Chapter 1)
Activity 2	Student Motivation Checklist (based on Chapter 2)
Activity 3	Self-knowledge – the role of learning styles (based on Chapter 3)
Activity 4	The motivational environment (based on Chapter 4)
Activity 5	The Interactive Observational Styles Index (based on Chapters 3–7)
Activity 6	Quick Learning Styles Summary
Activity 7	The Learning Environment – an audit (based on Chapters 4, 8 and 9)
Activity 8	Revision Strategy 1 – organisation (based on Chapter 5)
Activity 9	Revision Strategy 2 – mind mapping (based on Chapter 5)
Activity 10	Framework for background knowledge (based on Chapter 6)
Activity 11	Social learning preferences (based on Chapter 7)
Activity 12	Classroom management (based on Chapter 8)
Activity 13	Action plan for Special Needs
Activity 14	School Ethos Checklist (based on Chapter 9)
Activity 15	Stress proofing the school (based on Chapter 9)
Activity 16	Stress proofing the teacher (based on Chapter 9)
Activity 17	Six steps to good time management
Activity 18	Personal Stress Audit
Activity 19	Stress proofing the student (based on Chapters 8 and 9)
Activity 20	SNAPSHOT for learning
Activity 21	Reflection (based on Chapter 10)
Activity 22	My Personal Learning Profile (PLP 1)
Activity 23	My Personal Learning Plan (PLP 2)
Activity 24	My Supports
Activity 25	My Study Plan

Section 2

Staff Development – PowerPoint Presentation

Contents: i)   Motivation
           ii)   Learning Styles
           iii) Learning Environment
           iv) Memory
           v)   Tasks and Expectations
           vi) Social and Emotional Factors
           vii) Effective Schools
           viii) Reflection

Acknowledgements

I wish to acknowledge a number of people and organisations that provided assistance with this book. Dr Sionah Lannen and Colin Lannen of the Red Rose School in St. Annes on Sea, Lancashire, UK, for providing a model of effective practice; Fil Came of Learning Works for practical examples of motivation and effective learning; Shannon Green for assistance with the visual summaries at the end of each chapter and for reading and commenting on drafts, and to both Shannon Green and Corey Zylestra at REACH Learning Center in North Vancouver, Canada, for advice, support and encouragement. Also to Gad Elbeheri of the CCET in Kuwait for his insights into managing a motivating learning environment.

I also wish to acknowledge the appreciation and the interaction I have experienced with audiences I have spoken to all over the world. I have presented talks and seminars to thousands of teachers, school management, professionals and parents in over 40 countries – this interaction has done a great deal to shape my thinking.

It is always heartening for authors to receive positive responses from readers and I feel fortunate in this respect as it is these responses which have motivated and stimulated me into writing this book. I hope it helps to fulfil the need among teachers to learn more about motivation and effective learning and to ensure that all students everywhere realise their potential to become effective and motivated learners.

Dr Gavin Reid
Edinburgh, Scotland, UK

About the author

Dr Gavin Reid is a prolific author and his work has won and been nominated for a number of educational awards. He has written 18 books and has lectured to thousands of professionals and parents in 40 countries. He has also had books published in Polish, Italian, Arabic, Hebrew and Slovak.

He is an experienced teacher, author and educational psychologist. He is currently a senior lecturer in Educational Studies at Moray House School of Education, University of Edinburgh; a director of the Red Rose School in Lancashire, UK; consultant psychologist at Reach Learning Center in Vancouver, Canada; project consultant to the Centre for Child Evaluation and Teaching (CCET) in Kuwait; and a trainer and educational consultant for Learning Works International.

He is also an advisor to the board of the Canadian Academy of Therapeutic Tutors (CATT) and on two editorial boards for international journals on dyslexia and on reading. He has been external examiner to 14 universities world wide.

Introduction

This book is directed to all those concerned with the experience of learning and demonstrates how teachers in particular can make learning more efficient and effective for all students.

The key message of this book is that motivation is crucial for effective learning and this develops from an understanding of the learning process. That process relates to the complete learning experience – the learner's preferences, the expectations placed on the learner, the task, the teaching process, learning strategies, the resources and the learning environment. The role of management and school ethos are also considered in this book as school systems can have implications for motivation and effective learning.

This book is about learning and principally about helping teachers to help learners build a solid foundation for learning – a foundation that will assist in the development of motivation and effective learning and promote learner independence. The book is not a 'pick and mix' collection of ideas on learning, but is about planning for learning, developing the foundations for learning and learner autonomy. The book lays the foundations for lifelong learning. The foundations of learning, the learning plans, the emotional and cognitive factors and how learning is presented and assessed, as well as the fundamental issue of motivation, are all crucial elements of this book.

How to use this book

Some key points are highlighted throughout the book – ideas to try in the classroom that will allow the reader to have a complete matrix of the processes involved in independent and effective learning. Additionally, the CD Rom included with this book will provide many tried and tested strategies related to each of the chapters. A visual overview is included at the end of each chapter. This supplies a global and visual picture for visual learners. The Key points of a chapter can be found at the start of each chapter.

The key message of this book

The CD Rom attached to this book provides practical activities related to key points in each chapter of the book. This is important as whilst the reader can contextualise each of the ideas in this book to their own practice, it is important to receive some examples and guidance on how this might be achieved.

The key message of this book is encapsulated in the statement that learners need every opportunity to take responsibility for their own learning and that effective learning is not only an individual responsibility, but a whole-school responsibility. Learning should be fun – it should be social and interactive. It is hoped that the messages contained in this book promote that fun in learning and encourage a climate of success amongst learners which importantly is shared between all the staff in all learning establishments.

An overview of the book

The first chapter provides an outline and a rationale for the book in order to establish the importance of the foundations of learning and of the learning experience for developing effective learning.

Chapter 2 focuses on motivation. The simple reality is that effective learning will not take place if the learner does not want to learn. Quite often a teacher has to think of ways of motivating learners. But learning is more effective if a learner can develop self-motivation. This is discussed further in Chapter 2.

Chapter 3 highlights the importance of self-knowledge. It is crucial that learners develop their own way of tackling problems. Certainly they will need guidance, but a teacher's method of learning may not be the same as their students. It is important to recognise diversity in learning and to acknowledge that no two learners will learn in the same way. It is also important to recognise that there is no 'right' way to learn – learning is very much an individual preference. This chapter will examine different learning styles and show how learning styles and learning preferences can be used to develop effective learning skills. There will also be a focus on the need for learning styles to be seen within a whole-school context.

Chapter 4 looks at the learning environment. It is important to recognise that the learning environment plays a crucial part in effective learning. Learners have to be aware of the impact different environments can have on their learning.

Chapter 5 focuses on memory and looks at aspects of recalling, revising, reviewing and reflecting. The emphasis will be on using information to enhance understanding. This latter point – understanding – is crucial as this is the key to an efficient and effective memory.

Chapter 6 looks at the type of tasks that can be developed to help learners and will provide examples of tasks for different types of learners. Some learners such as those with dyslexia or attention difficulties will require a highly structured task. They will need a framework to follow. If they do not have this they may miss the point of the task, go off track and therefore will not display their full understanding of the task. An important point to consider is that a structure can usually benefit all learners. Learning should be fun. If you observe children in a nursery school the excitement and the enjoyment of learning are very obvious. Yet when you look at the same children ten years down the line they are quite different – for many the excitement will have gone out of learning and they will often perceive learning in a stressful and disaffected manner. The research indicates that learners function more effectively in a stress-free environment. It is important therefore to consider the social and emotional aspects of learning and to ensure that learners benefit from rewarding and stress-free learning experiences.

This is the key theme of Chapter 7 which focuses on preparing the 'whole school' emotionally for the learning experiences – this can be done through emotional literacy programmes and through social leaning activities. There will also be an emphasis on managing stress – both organisational stress and individual stress – in this chapter.

Chapter 8 looks carefully at managing learning in the classroom situation. This chapter will include suggestions for behaviour management, the need to be proactive and the type of support that can be beneficial for students with additional needs. This chapter will also suggest 20 key principles for classroom management.

This is followed by Chapter 9 which highlights key aspects of an effective school. This chapter takes a whole-school approach and looks at learning from this perspective. The implication is that classroom learning will be more effective if the school itself is an effective school. This is an institutional responsibility and this chapter will discuss the role of school climate, school ethos and school management.

Chapter 10 will provide some reflections on the key issues and strategies contained in the book. This also emphasises the importance of reflection in learning.

The Appendix will provide information on sources of support and further reading. It is important that readers can contextualise the messages of this book for their own learning context and the last chapter on 'reflection' will encourage readers to translate some of these into their own teaching and learning situations.

The foundations of learning

This chapter will describe some of the basic principles of learning and will provide a foundation for the book. It will comment on:

- the importance of developing independent learning

- the need to consider the whole child – including the social and environmental aspects as well as cognitive factors

- the need to recognise individual differences amongst learners

- the importance for learners to develop their own learning strategies and to be able to adapt these to different learning situations

- a recognition of the diversity among learners in relation to cognitive differences and learning experiences

- the role of learning styles in the classroom

- the theoretical background underpinning learning strategies, including the metacognitive aspects of learning and particularly based on the work of Vygotsky and Bruner.

Planning for learning

One of the most discouraging and disappointing comments teachers often hear from students is 'I have been up every night for months studying and I still failed the exam!' This happens so often and teachers, and of course parents, immediately sympathise with the student; and so they should. There is nothing more demoralising than not obtaining a fair reward for your efforts and it is for that reason I have written this book. Its aim is to inform teachers on learning habits and strategies based on individual needs and preferences.

This will help to encourage students to develop their own effective learning techniques so they can maximise their time efficiently and be rewarded for their effort.

It needs to be recognised of course that learning is not only about passing exams – that is certainly part of learning, but it is not the main aim. One of the problems with books that aim to help students pass exams is that the reader is bombarded with a plethora of strategies that might, or might not, work for that individual. What is often omitted are the foundations of learning – the building blocks that can help learners to become aware of their own learning preferences and about how to use these effectively in new learning situations.

It is necessary to help learners develop independent and autonomous learning skills. Books on study skills often disempower rather than empower the learner, by being too prescriptive. This can facilitate an over-dependence on what are essentially other people's strategies, and when these do not work learners will immediately feel they are doing something incorrectly. It is for that reason that we need to look at the learning process and more importantly how that process can be maximised and personalised for individual learners.

★ **KEY POINT**

Provide a summary of key points at the beginning of a text. This is important and is emphasised in the example above relating to this book. This helps the reader select those aspects of a book that are most appropriate. Additionally it also provides a means of recapping and checking that the whole text has been understood. Summaries should have key points and these will emphasise the importance of each part of the text.

Developing effective learning

Developing effective learning is like building a house. A house consists of individual bricks and requires solid foundations otherwise it will collapse when under strain. Learning is the same – if the founwdations for learning are not in place the learner will have difficulty when coming across new and challenging learning tasks.

A plan is essential for building a house. The builder does not pick up bricks as he/she goes along and slots them in. No – every brick and every component have each a place in the plan of the house. Nothing is left to chance. It is the same for learning. Nothing should be left to chance – it is important to plan so that the learner is ready and prepared for new and more challenging learning tasks. Yet in practice what we find is that perhaps the curriculum is planned and the teaching is usually planned and but the learning (namely, how a learner interacts with the new material) is not. In practice it is often left to chance!

Feeling secure – the heart and mind

For most people their home is a place of security. Inside it is equipped to make the people staying there secure and comfortable. The same principles should adhere to learning. It is important that a learner feels comfortable when learning which means the learning environment has to be right for that learner. The environment is an important consideration in learning and is discussed later in this book.

Appearance

We often judge the quality of a house by its appearance. Presentation both inside and outside is important. We may well be able to draw some conclusions about the owners if for example the garden is untidy, the outside needs painting and the curtains are hanging off their rails! Similarly we need to consider the manner in which the learning task is met and presented. How the task appears to the learner can be important. Some learners can switch off within seconds of seeing a task because it looks too formidable; the sentences are too long or the vocabulary is too complex. How learners react to a task can tell us much about them, their learning styles and their learning preferences.

Developing independent learning

Independent learning is one of the most important indictors that effective learning has taken place. If learners can work independently this means that they have fully under-stood the task. They are able to make decisions on how to tackle new learning based on their background understanding and their capacity for independent learning. The key issues here are learning resourcefulness and independence in learning. 💿 (See CD Rom Activity 1.) The learner who repeatedly asks someone rather than tries to work through the solution themselves can in fact be:

- Off-loading the pressure of thinking to someone else, or at least sharing it. For some learners this is important as they need to articulate the problem before they can even begin to solve it.

- Perhaps they may be utilising the skills of others because they have not acquired those skills themselves. They simply do not have the 'know how' to think through the problem and work out the steps themselves.

Dependence and independence – the role of the system

A question that should be asked is – does the education system promote independent learning? Many people are unable to work through a problem themselves. This may be due to the type of education they received because this education shaped their learning preferences and made them dependent on others. In recent years there has been a more obvious thrust towards problem-solving activities in the curriculum. This involves making decisions and thinking about and justifying decisions. This is the key to independent learning and often this is embedded in the learning ethos in a school.

★ **KEY POINT**

Encourage learners to develop an understanding of the learning process and how they can become more effective learners through tackling problems. Many learners do not get enough experience with this type of activity and it is those learners whose main strategy in solving learning problems is to ask someone. They are part of a dependency culture and it might be difficult for these learners, without support, to break out of this and become independent learners.

Learning takes all of you

There has been a great deal of attention paid to different styles of learning – visual, auditory, kinaesthetic and tactile – and the assumption is that each person has a preferred mode of learning. This may well be the case for some and is usually referred to as one's learning style.

A useful definition of learning styles is that it is a relatively stable indicator of a person's cognitive and environmental preferences for learning. This can include the visual, auditory and kinaesthetic, as well as factors such as attention and memory and environmental aspects such as time of day, light, background noise and classroom seating arrangements. It is important however to ensure that one does not view learning style as an inflexible and fixed way of processing information. It is not a blood group! Yet for many a knowledge of their learning style can help significantly in learning and particularly in tackling tasks that can be demanding.

However, there are now significant research studies that indicate that learning is a total experience. All the modalities are important, with emotional and environmental factors as important as cognitive learning factors. Similarly it is important for some learners to work in groups. For some this might be the only way they can function as a learner. This point will be developed in more detail later in this book.

★ **KEY POINT**

Ensure that learning involves all the senses, namely the visual, auditory, kinaesthetic and tactile. Many people have a preferred modality and need to use this when they are learning new material. If a learner is very visual then he/she may not be able to listen to instructions for any length of time as listening focuses on the auditory modality. It is also important to recognise the role of the social and emotional experiences of a learner. This could determine how well they will perform in groups and how they may react to working independently.

Individual differences and diversity

It is crucial to acknowledge individual differences in learning. This includes students with identifiable disabilities as well as learners who have no disabilities. It is too easy and simplistic to suggest, for example, if a learner has dyslexia, or ADHD that one particular approach should be followed. Students will have individual preferences and that includes those with dyslexia and ADHD or any other category of difficulty.

It is important to cater for the diverse needs of students and to acknowledge intellectual, cognitive and cultural differences, taking on board this diversity when planning for learning.

The importance of theory

There are a number of different theories that attempt to explain how children learn. There are however some common strands that need to be considered by a teacher. These include:

- **Understanding:** a learner needs be able to understand the requirements of the task.

- **Planning:** a learner needs to be able to identify the key points and work out a learning plan.

- **Action:** a learner needs to have the resources and the skills to carry out the task.

- **Transfer of learning:** previous learning should help to provide a plan and strategies for tackling new tasks.

Who takes responsibility if a task cannot be achieved by a learner? It might be said that the task is too difficult and is beyond a learner's current capabilities.

If that is the response then a significant opting-out is taking place. It is not a learner's responsibility – it is a teacher's responsibility to ensure that a task is achievable. It is only through ensuring that tasks are achievable that potential failure will be minimised. There are a number of considerations that need to be taken into account and these start by planning well before the task is presented.

The key issues include the need to:

1   anticipate the barriers a student may encounter;

2   accumulate some knowledge of learners' individual learning preferences;

3   differentiate the task through presentation and through outcome;

4   gradually assist a student in taking responsibility for their own learning and being able to monitor their own progress.

Some key points therefore that need to be considered throughout this book include:

■ **Learning is a process and this process takes place over time**. Some students will require more time than others and flexibility needs to be built into the learning process for that reason.

■ **Learning requires a period of consolidation**. This means that for some students over-learning is necessary. They may appear to have learnt something new – but they may not have consolidated that new piece of learning. For example, you open a new online account with a department store and have to key in a user, name and password. If you do not use the account for some time you may forget or confuse the details you have inserted. This is because you have not used this information and therefore you do not have automaticity in the use of that information. The general rule is that if you do not use it, you lose it, unless of course you have acquired automaticity. But this can only be achieved through a period of consolidated learning. A good example is when you are teaching a child to spell a word. You can teach him/her for an entire week and by the end of it the word seemingly is learnt and the child is able to spell it correctly. After a few days break however you may find that the child has not retained the ability to spell that word. For that child a week may not have been long enough. Usually children have to use a word they are learning over a period of time before it can become consolidated.

■ **Learning is more effective when the content is familiar**. This seems quite obvious but it means that the content has to be made familiar to the learning if a student does not already have some degree of familiarity with it. One of the most effective means of achieving this is through pre-task discussion. This can ensure that the key concepts and the main ideas are understood. Some learners need to engage in this before they can even think of tackling a task independently.

■ **Over-learning needs to be planned**. Over-learning should not happen by accident, it needs to be planned. It is important to present the materials that have to be learned in different teaching contexts and also to present them over a period of time. This enhances the opportunities for retention and understanding.

■ **Learning is holistic**. Learning involves social and emotional factors as well as thinking and learning skills. For that reason there will be sections in this book that will focus on 'feelings' – emotional factors – and getting the environment right for learning. Environmental aspects of learning as well as mood and emotional readiness are very individual factors, but it is important that these are built into learning programmes and are addressed in the identification of learning styles.

■ **Learning is long term**. Learning is long term in many ways – not only does one need a period of consolidation to ensure learning has been acquired but learning does not stop, it is a lifelong activity. Again it is important that everyone is equipped with their own handbook of learning, to know themselves as a learner and to appreciate and recognise the most effective methods for them. Yet surprisingly the actual process of learning does not occupy much space in a crowded school curriculum.

Learning theory – the Zone of Proximal Development

This book is not meant to be an analysis nor a discussion on learning theory. It is important however to recognise that learning theory can have an impact on teaching and learning. Vygotsky's social constructivist theory and particularly aspects relating to the Zone of Proximal Development and the need to 'scaffold' learning have influenced classroom practices. Both these concepts are important for effective learning and both provide an analysis of the learning process. Vygotsky (1986) summarised this in the following way. What the child can do in co-operation today, he can do alone tomorrow. Therefore the only good kind of instruction is that which marches ahead of development and leads it: it must be aimed not so much at the ripe as at the ripening functions.

Vygotsky theory (1962: 78) can be summarised as follows:

- There can be a significant difference, at any stage in learning, between what a learner can achieve unaided as compared with the situation where there is an instructor/teacher present interacting with that learner.

- Vygotsky also suggested that at any moment there are some skills/knowledge that are attainable, given a learner's current knowledge at that time. Simultaneously some skills/knowledge **cannot** be accessed by the learner because he/she is not at a stage of preparedness to understand/absorb/implement these new skills or knowledge.

- The set of skills that are currently attainable according to Vygotsky can be described as the 'Zone of Proximal Development' (ZPD). This means that one of the key aspects of effective teaching is to ensure that a learner is presented with tasks within his/her ZPD.

- The procedure called scaffolding describes the processes of support that are needed to allow a learner to reach the next stage in his/her learning. This process is like a series of steps that help the learner reach the required level. The important point is that these steps facilitate understanding rather than competence. What one is trying to achieve is understanding – it is possible for someone to appear competent in a skill without having underlying understanding. It is this understanding that is crucial for being able to acquire new learning more easily. The understanding refers to both the content of what is to be learnt, as well as the actual processes and scaffolds necessary for effective learning.

Some suggestions for scaffolding are shown below:

- **Introductory activities:** these are essential lead-in activities and provide the means for understanding new learning. Pre-task discussion is one example of a lead-in activity.

- **Recap activities:** these are important for effective learning. Recap activities should highlight the key points. Many students have real difficulty in recapping and can find it hard to identify the main points in a new piece of learning.

Recapping is probably underrated and underused in learning. It is also important to allow time to revisit previous work and draw on prior knowledge.

- **Bridge-building activities:** one of the most essential aspects of learning is the skill in making connections. Effective learning depends to a great extent on how readily a learner can make connections between the ideas and the content of the material to be learnt and also between the new learning and previous learning.

- **Using to prevent losing:** it is important that a learner has opportunities to practise the knowledge and skills gained from new learning. It is this practice that leads to automaticity and it is automaticity that demonstrates that the leaner has acquired competence and will be able to use this new skill to help with new learning.

- **Consolidation activities:** these are important and each lesson, or period of learning, needs to finish with a summary of possible consolidation activities. This is essentially over-learning and is part of the process that can lead to automaticity. Scaffolding therefore is the process by which a teacher has to respond appropriately to a learner's behaviour in a learning situation. It is a form of guided participation and both the interactions and these actions shape children's acquisition of the new material. An important element of this learning process is self-reflection and evaluation. This is the essence of metacognition – namely, self-reflecting on how learning has been tackled.

Bruner (1965) also has had a significant impact on education and on our understanding of the learning process (see also Donaldson 1978). One of the key principles advocated by Bruner is that of readiness. This implies that teaching must be concerned with the experiences and contexts that make a student willing and able to learn. A student needs to be cognitively and emotionally ready for new learning.

Bruner also suggests that teaching needs to be structured so that it can be easily grasped by a student. This learning organisation should be done at the planning stage so that the structure is in place before learning commences. At the same time, Bruner states that often we do not give children credit for what they are capable of and as such we can unwittingly restrict their progress. He further suggests that teaching should be designed to facilitate extension and/or to fill in the gaps in a student's understanding.

It is this factor of extending learners and going beyond their current levels that is crucial for effective learning. The work of Vygotsky and Bruner is important, and that of Piaget also (1954, 1970), in helping to determine the supports within the learning process that can be used by a learner and also in helping to realise and extend the potential of all learners.

These factors also help us become aware of the notion of 'learned helplessness'. If the supports and the scaffolds are not in place then a student may fail in a task and this failure can be translated into learned helplessness. That is when a learner perceives his own abilities as not being sufficient to carry out the task without support – or indeed even with support. That is why it is important to recognise the role both of the foundations of learning and of the teacher–learner interaction throughout the learning process. This should help to equip learners with a self-knowledge of learning and it is this which promotes independence in learning.

Key Points to Remember

- The need to recognise an individual learner's personal learning preferences.

- The importance of encouraging learners to become independent learners, so they have control over the learning task and the learning situation.

- Learning should not be left to chance. It has to be planned for in order for the learning to be effective. This planning also needs to consider the individual preferences of a learner.

- The aim is to equip learners with the new skills that would enable them to know **how** to tackle a task using these skills, their own preferences and their previous knowledge.

Chapter 1 At a Glance
Foundations of Learning

Helping teachers build a strong foundation for learners.

Learning			
Task	Environment	Resources	
Independence	Individual	School Climate	Learning Preferences
Plan for Learning	Motivation	Equip Learner	Self-reflection

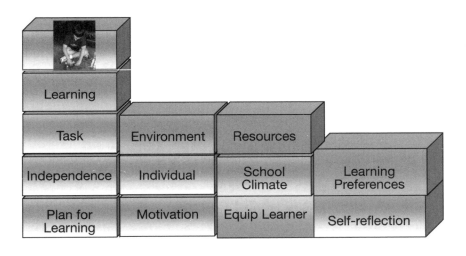

Key Points

Emotional

Self-knowledge

Metacognition

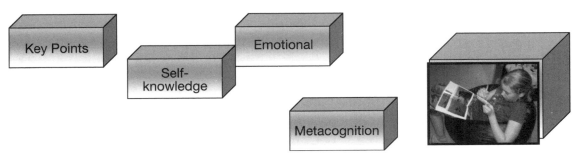

Effective learning stems from an understanding of the learning process

Motivation to learn

Motivation is a key factor in successful learning and this chapter will focus on strategies to develop motivation. These will include:

■ setting goals, short-term targets and rewards,

■ the importance of intrinsic motivation

■ an acknowledgement that motivating children to learn is not the responsibility of one teacher, but incorporates the whole-school ethos and school climate.

Ideally motivation should be intrinsic – that is, a learner is self-motivating. To achieve this however a learner needs to have a desired goal and some determination to succeed. Children who experience barriers to learning, such as those with dyspraxia and dyslexia, can find motivation challenging as repeated failure will result in serious de-motivation. As referred to in the previous chapter, this state is often referred to as 'learned helplessness'. It is crucial that a learner does not reach this state and for that reason early success is important when tackling new tasks. It is also important that both the extrinsic (rewards) and the intrinsic (self-motivation) are taken into account in the planning of learning.

Several years ago I spoke at a conference with an intriguing title – Motivating to Learn, Learning to Motivate (RTLB Conference, Dunedin, New Zealand, 2003). The conference organisers really ought to have been congratulated for that title – they got it right. These two phrases, *Motivating to Learn* and *Learning to Motivate*, are crucial for effective learning. A car will not run without fuel, children will not learn without motivation – the 'fuel' of learning. At the same time not all children are intuitively and intrinsically motivated to learn. Some children need to be motivated and a teacher has to develop the means and methods to enable and facilitate this motivation.

Motivation by task

For many, the sight or indeed the thought of certain types of tasks can be sufficient to de-motivate them. There is therefore an onus on teachers to develop achievable tasks. This in turn can be the first major barrier that has to be overcome in order to maintain motivation. Some learners, if they have experienced repeated failure, will become totally de-motivated and will not want to engage in learning new material in any way at all. It is important that children can experience success before they become de-motivated.

It is for that reason that great care must be taken when developing tasks to ensure that these are motivating and importantly that a learner believes a task is achievable. It is necessary that a task is broken down into small steps and that every step represents an achievable and rewarding outcome for a learner.

Motivation by reward

Although rewards are useful they should be seen as a short-term strategy – a step towards self-motivation. Rewards are normally only successful in the short term and can help children who need a boost, particularly if they are finding a task challenging. Rewards must be also be achievable and learners must value rewards. Ideally, it is best if any reward is negotiated with a learner.

Social motivation – the influence of peer groups

The chapter on learning styles (Chapter 3) will show how some learners prefer to learn on their own whilst others need social interaction. Social interaction can be beneficial as it can help develop important social skills, such as turn taking and sharing and listening to other people's opinions. The process of helping and working with others can in itself be motivating. Group dynamics can be positive or negative and it is important to ensure that the composition of a group is beneficial to all. A constructive and positive group working harmoniously can be a significant motivator. A motivated group will be able to pull the resources of all the members of the group together and this can be a strong motivating force.

Motivation by feedback

Every learner needs feedback to ensure he/she is on the correct path, but feedback is often used as a means of grading or correcting. Using feedback in this way teachers run the risk of de-motivating the learners. It is important that feedback is seen as different from correcting work. Feedback should be continuous and formative and should not necessarily come at the end of a task. Moreover, feedback should be positive or framed in a positive manner.

Motivation by achievement

It can be quite illuminating talking to a group of high achievers. Some very successful learners are not aware of their own success. They may measure or perceive success in a different way to others. A student who is accustomed to obtaining straight 'A's may feel a failure if she/he obtains a 'B' – yet this can be a highly commendable grade. The 'must be best' syndrome is quite widespread in today's competitive society and although this has some positive elements it can be seen as a very risky strategy and one that can place enormous pressure on the learner.

The key point here is what do we mean by achievement? Achievement is not necessarily reaching the goal set by the teacher. Achievement depends on the learner and their readiness for the task. If a person does not achieve then the task will need to be revised until they can achieve it! That is why the steps used in breaking down tasks are important.  (See CD Rom Activity 2.)

★ **KEY POINT**

Moving to intrinsic motivation

Intrinsic means within and intrinsic motivation is the desire to embark on a task stemming from within the individual. Learning will be more effective if children are intrinsically motivated and this will also facilitate independence in learning.

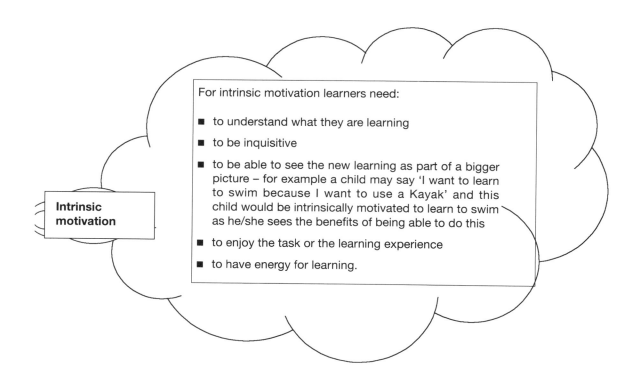

For intrinsic motivation learners need:

- to understand what they are learning
- to be inquisitive
- to be able to see the new learning as part of a bigger picture – for example a child may say 'I want to learn to swim because I want to use a Kayak' and this child would be intrinsically motivated to learn to swim as he/she sees the benefits of being able to do this
- to enjoy the task or the learning experience
- to have energy for learning.

Intrinsic motivation

> ★ **KEY POINT**
>
> One of the skills in teaching is being able to recognise learners' natural motivators – often learners may not be aware of these and it is teachers who have to recognise this and help students use their natural skills and resources.

The motivating environment

The environment has the potential to have a considerable impact on learning, but environmental preferences are very individual and depend a great deal on an individual's learning style. Whilst it is important to help an individual find the best learning environment for him/her, it is unrealistic to be able to accommodate every environmental preference in a classroom. However some effort can be made to ensure that the classroom environment caters for a range of preferences.

This is shown in the example below:

quiet reading corner   social area/windows
small lamp

book/library   main work area   communal discussion area

The motivated school

As indicated earlier in this chapter motivation is a whole-school responsibility – and that particularly includes the school management. It is important that motivation is embedded within a school's ethos. Often a school's motto can have a deep and motivating message, such as is shown in the example overleaf.

(Courtesy of Red Rose School, St Annes on Sea, Lancashire, UK)

It is also important that motivation is seen in all aspects of school and not only in its achievements. One of the ways of achieving this is through collaboration between staff in a school and parents. This helps to ensure there is a common thread running through the activities of the school and can help staff to develop consistent motivating materials and strategies.

Twenty four strategies for motivation

These strategies for motivation are described below:

1   Encourage diversity in learning styles

■ Children's learning patterns are often the result of how they were taught and the learning environment and ethos of schools. For some children this is perfectly satisfactory as their styles and preferences match those of their schools. For others however this may not be the case. For that reason it is important to encourage diversity in children's learning preferences. This can be done by offering them choice and giving them the opportunity to utilise their own learning style in the classroom. Some mediating factors that can influence the use of learning styles are culture, school climate, teacher and parent expectations, teaching style and classroom norms and practices. It is therefore important to reflect on the above and ensure that flexibility is used to encourage diversity.

2 Encourage creativity

■ It is interesting to reflect on the fact that many creative people can only take control of their own learning after they leave education. Many fail at school, or certainly do not shine. This is because the examination system often does not encourage creativity. There are certainly signs that progress is being made in this area but often the pace of learning, to ensure that all examinable areas of the curriculum are covered, is fast. This means that there is little scope for digressing and indeed for encouraging creativity. For many learners creativity is the principal motivating factor. For example the young, rising pop singer who is directed by a record company to record covers by other artists all the time may soon tire of this and become de-motivated. Artists in particular need to be encouraged to use their creativity and this can in fact apply to all learners. Many when asked if they are creative would quickly reply 'no' because they have not had the opportunity to be creative.

3 Ensure success with small achievable steps

■ Success is an essential factor for motivation and for successful learning. It is a teacher's responsibility to ensure that a learners meet with success. If success is not evident then a task has to be further differentiated. Most learners take to learning new information in steps, although holistic learners do need to have an overview of the whole area first. The key point is to ensure that each of the steps is achievable and to ascertain that knowledge of a child's learning style and previous knowledge is available.

4 Provide feedback to students about their own personal progress

■ Progress is personal – progress for one may not be progress for someone else. It is important that the criteria for progress are not generalised but instead should be individualised. Once it has been decided what exactly constitutes progress for an individual this should be discussed and negotiated with them. Then personal goals can be established and progress more easily identified.

5 Learners need to believe in their own abilities

■ Self-belief is crucial if one is to accomplish any degree of success and motivation, yet often the education system is geared to select and to grade. These factors can totally wipe out any element of self-belief, so it is important to recognise and acknowledge any achievements – no matter how small they may seem to others. These can be huge for the individual learner. Even those who seem to have achieved a great deal of success – in the classroom or on the playing field – still need and rely on positive feedback to ensure that they can believe in their own abilities. It is often those who seem to have achieved a great deal who have a sur-prisingly low level of self-belief. This can be because they are not receiving the positive feedback they actually need. The common perception might be that these children do not need it because they know they are successful. The key point here is not to take this for granted and assume that some successful learners do not need positive and continuous feedback and encouragement in order for them to develop and maintain self-belief.

6   Acknowledge the individual styles of each child

■ This is important although it can be challenging in today's inclusive classrooms. If a young person is made aware of his/her learning style this can set them up for independent learning at home and beyond school.

7   Ensure a task is age and interest related

■ It is too easy, particularly with learners who have reading difficulties, to provide them with a text that may be at their reading level but not at their interest level. Obtaining age-appropriate materials for learners with reading difficulties is essential in order to develop motivation. Many publishers now provide reading materials that are high on interest but have a lower level of vocabulary (Reid 2007).

8   Use observation to begin with to get to know the learning and environmental preferences of the children in your class

■ Before developing materials for a class it is important that some knowledge of the individuals within the class is acquired. One of the most effective ways of doing this is through informal observation. The headings below can be used to acquire information on each child. For each of the headings you are asking how the learner deals with each category. For example how does he/she organise information? In what type of learning situations do they attend best? How do they interact with others in the class – is it a positive interaction? What type of factors motivate them to learn? The headings below can be used flexibly to obtain any type of information that can be useful.

a) Organisation

b) Attention

c) Sequencing

d) Interaction

e) Self-concept

f) Learning preferences

g) Motivation/Initiative

h) Independent learning.

These are developed in detail in Chapter 3 on learning styles and examples of possible responses are also shown below.

a) Organisation – *disorganised, loses possessions, notebook quite messy.*
b) Attention – *okay when doing something, easily distracted when listening and when working in groups.*

c) Sequencing – *has difficulty telling story in order, has difficulty with some mathematics problems.*

d) Interaction – *likes being the class clown.*

e) Self-concept – *has a lot of absence from schools, stomach aches and headaches, poor eye contact, does not have special friend but is often in company of other children.*

f) Learning preferences – *seems to be a visual and kinaesthetic learner.*

g) Independent learning – *has difficulty working on his own.*

9 Focus on the task and the curriculum

■ It is important not to focus too much on a learner – the nature of the task and the aims of the curriculum may have to be revised and this revision can make a difference between success and failure. It also prevents the onus from being on the learner and any consequent highlighting of their difficulties.

10 Use a range of learning styles in class lessons.

■ One of the signs of a well prepared classroom lesson is the extent of how it deals with a range of learning styles. Each lesson must have elements of the auditory, visual, tactile and kinaesthetic throughout. This is important to ensure that each child's learning style is accommodated for in some way.

11 Ensure lessons are meaningful

■ This may seem obvious but it is a common mistake to assume a child has the basic level of understanding to get maximum benefit from a lesson. It is important to check on his/her level of understanding and knowledge of the key concepts involved in the lesson. Only if the child has those levels of concepts will the lesson be meaningful.

12 Minimise pressure

■ Some children need some pressure to be motivated – for example, deadlines and competition. This should however be used carefully: too much pressure can result in total de-motivation as a student may not see a goal as achievable.

13 Group work

■ Working in groups can be a great motivator but at the same time it is important to ensure that the dynamics of a group provide a positive experience for all. It is too easy for one or more children to become passengers and feel 'left out'. In groups also it might be an idea to pair those children who get on well with each other together. Group work should be closely monitored and each group should report on their progress after short intervals.

14 Self-assessment

■ This is important as it helps children take control of their own learning. They should be encouraged to assess their own progress and this can be a motivator in itself. The key point is that they should be able to decide what they want to achieve and a teacher's role in this is to guide and monitor their progress. Self-assessment encourages self-reflection and this helps to develop higher order thinking skills.

15 Show progression

- It is important that a student is able to recognise progression. Some learners find this difficult and progression may have to be clearly shown to the learner. Self-assessment (discussed above) can be an important factor that combines with the need to show progression. A framework or even a checklist can help a learner note his/her progression.

16 Avoid potential stigma

- It is crucial that if a learner has any difficulty at all he/she is not singled out – even in a positive way – on account of this. Some difficulties require that a student receives extra time or special equipment and it is important that this is provided without any embarrassment to them.

17 Develop student responsibility

- The key to successful learning is student autonomy. This is important as it provides the learners with some control over their learning. It is this control that fosters responsibility and makes it possible for students to move from extrinsic to intrinsic motivation.

18 Encourage student choice

- This is part of the plan to provide learners with control and independence in learning. Choice in itself can foster independence and responsibility.

19 Give students responsibility for their own learning

- This is what we are aiming for in order to develop effective learning. The important point is that it is a gradual process and takes time to achieve. Responsibility can be given in small ways to begin with, but ultimately this should be the aim of all learning programmes.

20 Focus on learning as well as teaching

- Teachers can spend a considerable amount of time in planning lessons and ensuring that teaching programmes are well constructed. It is important however to focus on children's learning as well as teaching and to consider this in the preparation of materials. It is important to help a student prepare a learning plan for the task – this can be different from a teaching programme.

Example of a learning plan

Task – building a bridge

A learning plan would need to include a structure – this would help students understand the task and be able to follow through its different stages, including any opportunities for self-monitoring progress.

Learning Plan

    a) Make a list of the materials you will need to build a bridge.

    b) Then have a look at books in the library on bridges.

    c) Decide on the kind of bridge you want to build. Make a list of three possible types of bridges that you might consider.

    d) Go outside to survey and decide where the bridge will be built – give three reasons for this.

    e) Have a look at colours and styles and decide if you need any more materials.

    f) Make a list of each of the tasks and tick off each one from the list after completion.

    g) Reflection: What did you find difficult about this task? What did you find easy?

One of the key points about the learning plan is that it has reflection built into it. It is important that children see each task as a learning experience and that some of the strategies and techniques used throughout this experience can be used in future learning.

21 Involve the class in decisions

    ■ Children's motivation will be significantly enhanced if they have an opportunity to be involved in decisions. They need a sense of ownership over tasks and learning experiences. For that reason it is useful if they can be involved in decision making as much as possible.

22 Celebrate success

    ■ Children like to celebrate and often develop their own rituals and style of doing this – which can develop team spirit and enhance group motivation.

23 Use positive feedback

    ■ Feedback can be 'purely informational feedback about one's performance' but if the information communicates appreciation for the quality of work, then the verbal feedback can enhance intrinsic motivation.

24 Encourage self-evaluation

    ■ Ideally self-evaluation should be promoted as much as possible. This can minimise the need for teacher approval. Often a student can become dependent on teacher approval and this is essentially an extrinsic form of reward. It is important to shift to intrinsic reward and this can be an outcome of self-evaluation. It also indicates that a student has taken some responsibility for a task and should be able eventually to gain insights into the learning processes involved in it.

Key Points to Remember

- Motivation is a key factor in successful learning.

- Great care must be taken when developing tasks to ensure that they are motivating and importantly that a learner believes a task is achievable.

- A constructive and positive group working harmoniously can be a significant motivator.

- Feedback should be continuous and formative.

- Intrinsic motivation is important in order to promote independence in learning.

- The term 'the motivated school' indicates that motivation is a whole-school experience and the school climate and school ethos are important considerations.

- The nature of the learning experience should be acknowledged and used to promote motivation and independence in learning.

- It is important to acknowledge learning style and learning diversity as these can promote motivation.

- Self-assessment and self-monitoring should be developed as far as possible.

- It is important to encourage student responsibility when engaged in a task. This can give students a sense of ownership over the task and this in itself is a great motivator.

Motivation is key to successful learning

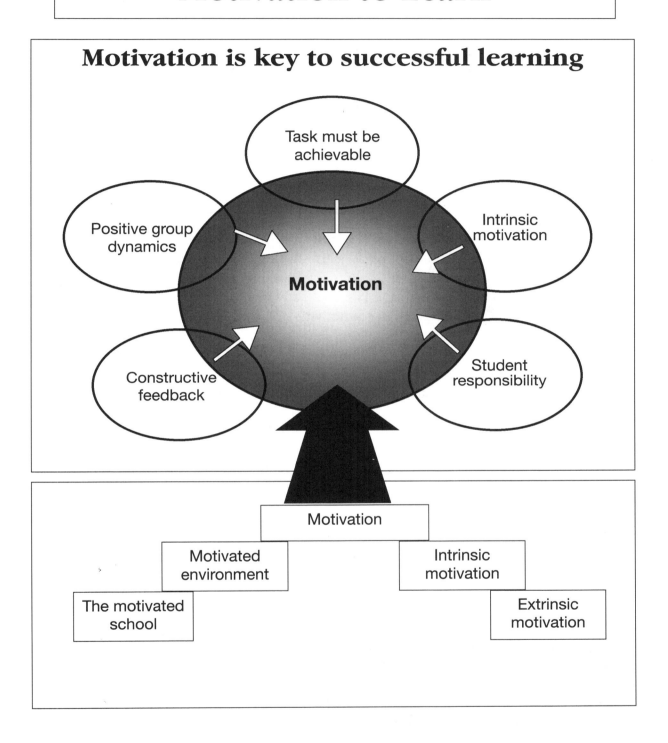

Self-knowledge – the role of learning styles

This chapter will provide examples of a range of learning styles and highlight how learning styles can be used to develop learning skills and promote effective learning. The suggestions made in this chapter on learning styles can be applied to all age ranges throughout the school. Practical activities relating to this are included in the CD Rom. (See particularly Activities 3, 4, 5, 6, 7 and 10.) The chapter will include:

- the use of different models of learning styles focusing on the learning environment, classroom observation and modality preferences

- guidance on the advantages and disadvantages of different learning styles for different types of tasks

- a focus on the need for learning styles to be seen within a whole-school context.

★ KEY POINT

It may be more useful to use the term 'learning preferences' rather than 'learning style'. One of the key points that should be made at the outset is that learning style is not a precise science. The identification of learning styles can be difficult and not all children have a clear preference, although a great many have. The importance of learning styles however can be more obvious when learners are facing a challenging task. In this type of situation self-knowledge, including knowledge of one's learning style and being able to adapt a task to meet an individual's learning style, can pay dividends. It may however be more useful to speak about learning 'preferences' rather than 'style' as the word 'preference' implies some flexibility whilst 'style' gives the impression of precision and innate characteristics.

The factors that can be associated with learning styles include:

- **Modality preference:** this refers to the preference for visual, auditory, tactile or kinaesthetic learning. Most learners will use all these modalities when tackling a task, but often learners can have a clear preference for one or two of these modalities.

- **Personality type:** some learners need to engage emotionally with the task. Some need to be quite adventurous when engaging in learning and may attempt tasks that can be quite challenging whilst others might be more cautious and reflective.

- **Social factors:** some learners need to work collaboratively with others. For some this social aspect is very important whilst others may need to tackle a task on their own.

★ **KEY POINT**

Learning styles and learning preferences need to embrace cognitive, social and personality factors. It can be misleading to view learning styles from a purely cognitive perspective. Although learning style does embrace how people think and process information, it is more than that. Learning itself is influenced by other factors such as the environment and social groupings and the personality of the learner. For example, some learners need to have a quiet environment whilst others need to have visual and auditory distractions.

Managing learning styles in the classroom

Managing learning styles in a classroom context can present a considerable challenge to teachers. One should not underestimate the difficulty in preparing teaching and learning materials that can meet the needs of the wide range of learning styles found in a classroom group. This diversity of learning styles can be met through differentiation and advance planning but these need careful consideration which should be built into lesson and curriculum plans as well as being part of the preparation of teaching resources.

The following sequence and tasks may be helpful.

1   Identify the learner's individual learning styles and learning preferences. This can be done through using some of the instruments shown in the CD Rom attached to this book ⊙ (see Activity 3) but it can also be achieved through observation.

2   Identify curriculum objectives.

3   Identify the series of tasks to meet these objectives.

4   Identify what measures will be used to indicate whether these objectives have been met.

5   Plan how the content can be differentiated to meet the different learning styles.

6   Identify resources that will be necessary to support the range of styles.

7   Identify and plan the classroom environment that can incorporate the range of styles.

8   Show how learners will be able to use their experiences to develop control over the learning processes through self-direction and self-assessment.

★ **KEY POINT**

The use of learning styles in the classroom should be planned well in advance as the range of learning styles to be accommodated should be included in lesson plans and curriculum objectives.

The learning environment

The learning and classroom environment has an important role to play in effective learning, so what are the key components of the learning environment? These are all the factors that influence the learning experience. This can differ in different cultures and in different classrooms. The important aspect is that as many of the environmental factors as possible should be considered.

The classroom – lighting

Lighting in the classroom is important as there is now considerable evidence that learners can be sensitive to different ranges and types of lighting. There is a general agreement that fluorescent lighting is not the most effective for the majority of learners. It is a good idea therefore to ensure that there are small table lamps in the classroom in quiet corners.

Windows

Natural lighting is the best for most children but at the same time too much can be distracting and ideally there should be a combination between natural and artificial light. For some detailed tasks and for some learners, particularly those with attention difficulties, too much natural light can be distracting.

Colour

Colour can have a profound effect on learners and can influence not only the learning experience but also people's moods and attitudes. The general view is that pastel colours are soothing and calming. Bold colours like bright red can be dramatic and depending on the learners and the task bold as well as tranquil colours can be used.

Wall display

Wall displays can be very powerful and great effort should be taken to ensure they convey the right messages to children, staff and visitors. Displays can be informative and they can convey a powerful message.

Wall displays can provide a message to the school and to visitors

Classroom walls can also be a teaching aid as the picture above shows. This is fun and a good activity for kinaesthetic and tactile learners. The picture below also shows how a child could identify with their classroom more easily by leaving a handprint.

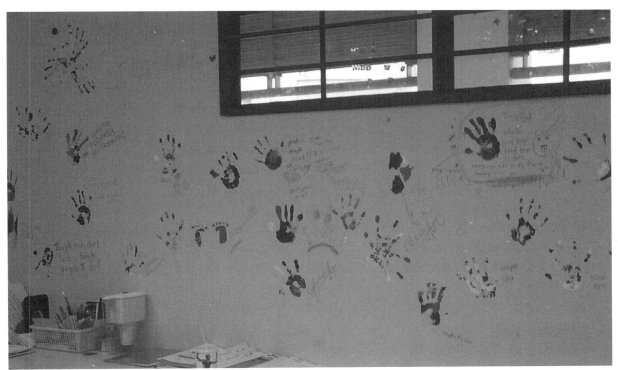

Walls can also be used for learning – this is useful for the tactile learner

29

Type of desks and desk layout

There are many different types of desk and classroom layout. Some desk arrangements however are fixed. This is not ideal for most learners although for children with attention difficulties it can minimise potential disruption. Ideally there should be some desks that are positioned to minimise distraction and others that can facilitate interaction. Classroom design is an important element in developing effective learning from a whole-school perspective.

Floor covering

The type of floor covering can be important as it can either minimise or maximise noise – ideally floors should be soft enough to muffle this and also comfortable enough for children if they wish to opt to sit on the floor whilst reading or when engaged in learning activities. This can reduce the restrictions often imposed by desks. In fact some children find it very difficult to sit at a desk. The floor can offer an alternative.

Location of teacher's base

Ideally in a classroom the teacher's base should not be obvious, yet in reality in most classrooms it occupies a central position. Some personal preferences can be seen here but if the classroom is designed to maximise learning then the teacher's base should be accessible but not necessarily occupying the central position in a classroom.

Range of activities/quiet corners

A classroom should be designed to ensure it is possible for children to engage in a range of different types of activities. This includes group work and quiet corners. The classrooms for younger children have usually cracked this one very well – most are designed with different activities in mind, yet when learning becomes more formal further up the school all these points are overlooked.

 KEY POINT

The classroom environment has a key role to play in facilitating effective learning. It is important to acknowledge all aspects of the environment and to attempt to provide a range of environmental choices in relation to lighting, noise and seating arrangements. Although it is appreciated that often space is limited in a classroom, it is important nevertheless to be aware of how the environment can impact on learners. It is also important to convey this to the learner so that at least he/she may be able to use this self-knowledge to create their optimum learning environment.

Other factors that can influence learning in the environment include:

- music
- noise
- accessibility to resources
- space for movement.

Sound

Sound can be one of the most distracting elements in learning. At the same time it has the potential to stimulate, invigorate and create. People react differently to different sounds and this needs to be considered in a learning environment.

Music

It is worthwhilst allowing some children to use headphones and monitor the output of their work when using background music. It is also important to experiment with different kinds of music, thereby ensuring that the right type of music is used for different activities.

Models of learning styles

Kolb's Experiential Learning Model

Kolb's 12-item learning style inventory yields four types of learner:

- divergers
- assimilators
- convergers
- accommodators.

Kolb's (1984) model is based on the concept of experiential learning and explores the cyclical pattern of learning from experience through 'reflection' and 'conceptualising' to 'action' and on to further 'experience.'

The key point is that different types of learner will use experiences in different ways. For example, whilst some learners see new experiences as a challenge others may see these as a threat. Some can accommodate to new experiences and assimilate these very quickly, whilst other types of learner need time to feel comfortable and to master new experiences.

★ KEY POINT

New learning experiences need to be carefully introduced to learners and knowledge of learning styles can inform this process. When new learning is being introduced it is best to introduce it using the learner's strengths – once the key ideas have been grasped then other means can be employed. This is particularly relevant if the new learning is challenging.

Given's five learning systems

Barbara Given (2002) has developed a comprehensive approach to learning styles by incorporating five learning systems.
These are:

■ emotional

■ social

■ cognitive

■ physical

■ reflective.

Learning systems according to Given are guided by hereditary factors but the environment determines people's responses to different learning situations. Key therefore is the interplay between an individual's learning system and a learner's environmental influences.

The educational implications of Given's learning systems are shown below:

■ **Emotional – self-direction**

Self-direction is an important factor in effective learning. The learner has to be sure of him/herself and have the confidence to take risks in learning. This is what one is hoping to achieve with all learners but some may never reach this level – yet can still be effective learners using other means of learning, for example from following instructions or working with others.

■ **Social – self-assurance**

In most cases learning takes place with others. This does not have to be so but often collaboration with others can enhance the result of the learning experience. To work constructively with others however requires a degree of confidence and self-assurance. It is important to help a learner develop this. Whilst some will feel comfortable working with others and will be able to do this instinctively, others may not. It is important to be aware of this and learners who do not have this self-assurance will need some support in this area. 💿 (See also CD Rom activity 11 on social learning preferences.)

■ **Cognitive – self-regulation**

Self-regulation refers to control over learning which is one of the most successful factors for effective learning. Control involves

a) *pacing learning* that is the speed at which one works particularly in meeting time deadlines.

b) *understanding of the task* often learners can embark on tasks without having a clear understanding of what has to be done, namely what the task is actually requiring the learner to do.

c) *having a clear plan* control over learning involves being able to plan and sequence the steps needed to complete the task.

d) *accessing resources* part of having control over learning is being able to know the most appropriate kind of resources and support to access.

■ **Physical – self-control**

Attention is one of the initial, key factors in learning. To a great extent this involves the physical control of attending and persisting with a task. Often learners with attention difficulties do not have good physical self-control and are characterised by their impulsive behaviour which can show evidence of a lack of physical self-control.

■ **Reflective – self-assessment**

Reflection on learning is an advanced stage in the learning process. Learners who are able to reflect on learning usually have well developed metacognitive skills. This means they are able to self-correct and to reflect on the task – and importantly how they have tackled, or will tackle, the task. Learners with reflective skills are usually efficient learners as they can use the same established strategies for new learning. They are more concerned with the 'how' rather than the 'what' of learning.

Learning as a process – the role of the curriculum

Learning should be seen as a process and Reid (2005) suggests that using learning styles as a teaching device may mean developing a broad-based approach to the ideas of a process curriculum and differential pedagogy. What this means is that the curriculum as we know it must be viewed from a different perspective. At present, the content of the curriculum seems to be the key component and indeed in many cases the only component. If learning style is to be seriously adopted then the planning of the curriculum will need to take into account the **how** question as well as the **what** and in addition actual teaching approaches will need to be different for different sets of learners. This has to be included and incorporated at the planning stage.

Whole-school planning

Whole-school planning is essential if learning styles are to be used effectively. Planning for learning styles requires a time commitment and the sharing of ideas and resources, but above all it must be taken on board by a school's management. This is because it must be introduced systematically and collaboratively, otherwise it will become a piece-meal initiative by a handful of teachers requiring significant effort. Moreover, when a child moves to another class – either as he/she progresses through primary school or in the different subject areas of secondary school – there may not be the necessary continuity in how that child's learning style is acknowledged.

Introducing learning styles into your school: A whole-school planning framework

- **Stage 1 – Setting the scene**
  Step 1 – Staff agreement
  This is important as successful implementation of learning styles requires the agreement of all those involved. Moreover, there needs to be a common agreement on the learning style approaches that are to be used and the implications of this for staff time and curriculum development.

- **Step 2 – Information on learning styles**
  There are many models of learning styles and different approaches to identifying these and using this information in classroom learning and teaching. Reid (2005) suggests there are over 80 instruments at least that can be used in the classroom. It is useful therefore to obtain a professional with some specialist knowledge to set the ball rolling and to give an introduction to some of the more appropriate styles and instruments that can be used.

- **Stage 2 – Planning for action**
  Step 3 – The appointment of a co-ordinator
  This is important and it can prove cost effective. Ideally it should be a teacher from within the school, but this responsibility can be shared with an outsider – perhaps the person who introduces the theme of learning styles in the staff development session.

Step 4 – Pilot learning style assessments
It might be useful to identify several different types of assessments that can be used – perhaps several in conjunction with each other. Once identified they can be piloted in different ages of children. It might be that one instrument is more appropriate for older rather than younger children, or vice versa. It is usually a good idea to develop and introduce an observational framework. (Such a framework is provided in the CD Rom included with this book.) An observational framework provides flexibility and can be adapted by each teacher to fit into the particular age and stage of children in a class.

Step 5 – Discuss results at staff meetings

This is important because it is essential that all staff are fully involved throughout all the stages of the process. There may well be some disagreement on the piloting stage and it is necessary that any disagreement is dealt with before the project advances.

■ **Stage 3 – The development stage**
Step 6 – The development of materials and teaching approaches

This is the crucial step which requires both a knowledge of learning styles and also a knowledge of the learners. But if this is seen as a group effort and not left to an individual teacher, then it will be more successful and there will be less of a burden on a few members of staff. Both materials and teaching approaches can be developed as a group and can be used in all classrooms. There are some common aspects that can also be discussed at this stage and these include wall and corridor displays and how learning styles can be used by the children in sport and additional curriculum activities.

■ **Stage 4 – Working together**
Step 7 – Informing parents and children

It is important that parents and children are aware that there is to be a focus on learning styles in the classroom. This helps them understand that learning styles and the learning environment can help solve problems and complete tasks more effectively. Children should be encouraged to talk about their style preferences and parents should also be made aware of this.

★ **KEY POINT**

All learning styles are valid and need to be respected. It is usually most beneficial if a child is supported to use his/her learning style more effectively rather than to attempt to change their style preferences.

■ **Stage 5 – Gathering together and reporting**

It is important that everyone involved has the opportunities to discuss their views and any concerns they have about implementing learning styles as a whole-school practice. For that reason the next stage is crucially important.

Step 8 – Implementation and evaluation

It is therefore important to monitor the implementation of learning styles and to have frequent evaluation meetings. The views of parents and children need to be included as well as those of the teachers.

Self-knowledge

One of the important aspects about learning styles is the opportunity it presents to facilitate self-knowledge. It can provide learners with a deeper self-awareness and a knowledge of their own particular learning preferences. This self-knowledge is necessary for developing independent learning skills and for utilising metacognitive skills. This is one of the spin-offs of using learning styles. By promoting this self-knowledge it helps learners to think and reflect on their own learning. This is essential for developing lifelong learning skills. Irrespective therefore of whether or not learning style is a precise science, it serves this useful purpose and can be a catalyst for self-analysis of the learning process.

Key Points to Remember

- Learning preferences may be a more useful term to use than learning styles and both need to embrace environmental and social factors as well as cognitive (processing) factors.

- Use a student's learning preferences to introduce new learning.

- View learning as a process not as a product. This has implications for curriculum development.

- Using a learning styles approach can assist students to develop self-awareness and a deeper understanding of the learning process.

Self-knowledge – The Role of Learning Styles

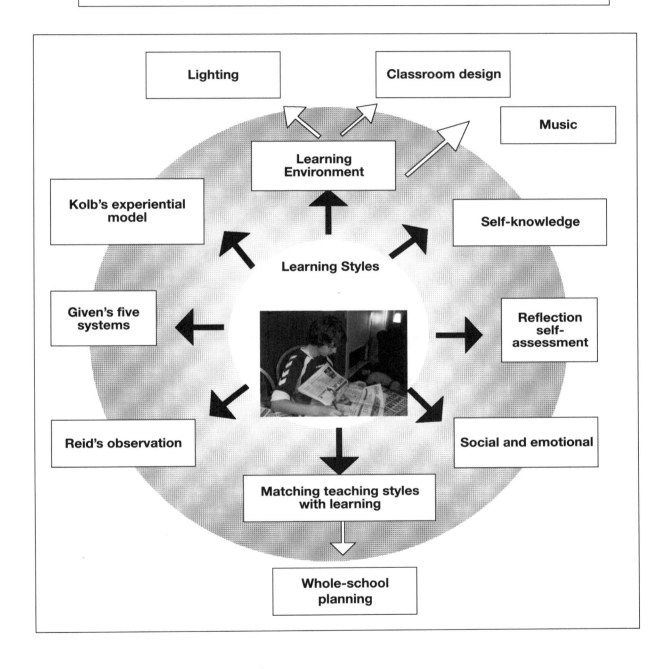

The learning environment

This chapter provides suggestions for maximising the learning environment to enhance learning. These factors include:

- the classroom design and layout

- environmental preferences of learners

- and *20 key factors* for consideration when planning a learning environment.

Classroom design

The classroom design and layout should try to accommodate for the diversity of students. The learning styles of students need to be considered – such as the effect of colour, sound, music and space. A good starting point is to perform a learning styles audit of the class to work out the range of preferences. From that it is possible to find the type of layout that might be suited to the majority of children in the class.

Learning environments

Some learning environments may be more suited to left hemisphere learners while others may be more suitable for right hemisphere learners. Left hemisphere learners generally prefer a quiet, formal and predictable environment, whilst right hemisphere learners prefer a more random, informal and usually visually and auditory stimulating environment.

Environmental preferences

Environmental preferences can be considered following discussion with a learner or through observation of them in different settings. It is useful to develop a framework for this (shown below). The idea behind this is that it is flexible and can be developed in relation to what you need to know in order to build a learning styles profile.

- **Organisation**

  This should focus on how the learner organises him/herself in terms of their cognitive organisation, as well as the materials they need to use. Cognitive organisation refers to the following:

  Input How information is initially processed and remembered in the short-term memory.

  Cognition How the information is understood, organised and retained for future use.

  Output How the information is presented by the learner to show the degree of mastery.

  In each of these cognitive stages the learner is required to organise the information he/she is processing. Some learners find this quite demanding and observing them as they go through these processes can provide insights into their learning preferences. This can in turn have implications for the learning environment.

- **Attention**

  It is important to assess the types of tasks that can promote, or indeed distract a learner. This can be seen by noting the environment and the type of tasks that can maintain and extend a learner's attention. It is also quite important to recognise when a learner's attention wavers and to note the tasks he/she is undertaking at that time.

- **Sequencing**

  In addition it is useful to note how a learner sequences information. This can give an indication in relation to their learning style and how the task should be presented for them. For example, does this learner prefer information in neat columns or in number form or do they prefer to learn in a more random manner?

- **Interaction**

  A great deal of information can be gleaned from the type of interaction that learners engage in and some environments can be more conducive to interaction than others. For example, if a learner's style is one that relies on interaction then the environment must be conducive to this and should permit a degree of freedom to allow such interaction.

- **Self-concept**

  The outcome of any learning activity can be determined to a great extent by the level of a learner's self-concept. Great effort needs to be made to ensure that a learner feels comfortable in an environment as otherwise it may affect his/her self-concept.

■ **Learning preferences**

It is important to profile students' learning preferences. When this is done it is also essential to consider the impact of the learning environment on individual learners. It is usually necessary to discuss this with a student in order to determine the most appropriate environment for his/her learning style.

■ **Motivation/initiative**

The nature and degree of motivation shown by the learning are important in determining the learning outcome. It should be noted whether this motivation stems from a learner's own initiative or whether they need to be prompted. This can have implications for the actual learning programme and the type of rewards whether intrinsic or extrinsic (see Chapter 2). (See also Activity 4 on the CD Rom on motivational preferences.)

■ **Independent learning**

Ideally this is what all learners should be striving for. Some can achieve this quite readily whilst others need a significant amount of support and structure to attain this. It is important to determine this so that a structure can be developed if necessary. It is also necessary to consider how such structures can be gradually removed, as it can be quite difficult to determine the balance between structuring support and removing that support.

20 key factors in the learning environment

1 **Layout**

The organisation of classroom furniture is an important consideration. If possible ensure a range of options for work bases, including individual desks with a degree of seclusion and open work spaces that can facilitate group work. It is important to consider that some learners need space and can feel confined if desks are too close together.

2 **The design of chairs and desks**

This must be considered as generally desks and chairs are designed for practicality and durability. Whilst these factors are necessary it is also important to consider the need for those factors associated with visual, aesthetic and comfort considerations.

3 **The position of a teacher's desk in relation to their students**

Traditionally the teachers desk is located at the front of the room and often in a prominent position. This however does not need to be the case. Much of course depends on how the classroom is designed but alternatives to this should be considered.

4 **The arrangement of students' desks**

There are many different ways of arranging learners' desks with rows and squares two of the most popular. It is a good idea to provide a choice for students. In this way it is possible to meet the learning and environmental preferences of most. Other methods of organising desks and chairs should also be tried out and student comments gathered on how they find the positioning of the classroom furniture.

5 Flexibility in being able to move and adjust the layout of the classroom

There is nothing quite as frustrating as having classroom furniture fixed – for example when desks are attached to chairs or they are fixed to the floor. Ideally the type of the classroom furniture should offer some flexibility so that it can be moved and rearranged.

6 The colour and design of a room

This is an important factor and there is a great deal of research on the effect of colour on individuals' moods and performance. Pastel colours tend to be soothing and this can be beneficial if students have a tendency to be hyperactive or distracted. Bright, bold colours such as orange and red can be stimulating but may over-stimulate in some cases. Some attention should therefore be paid to the colour and design of classrooms and it might be helpful to have a range of possible colours and designs in a room, for example pastel shades for a quiet corner and informal seating arrangements such as bean bags.

7 The amount of light

This is important – whilst some children learn best with minimal distractions others need visual stimulation. This means that for many light is important and natural light is preferable. It is a good idea to try to provide a mix of study areas – one with a lot of natural light and one with little light (perhaps using a table lamp). For some tasks such as those that focus on detail, like proof reading or mathematical calculations, reduction in visual stimulation may be preferable.

8 Predictability and routine

Children often obtain security from routine. It is therefore necessary to introduce some routine and sameness into the classroom environment. But at the same time children often become more stimulated by the unexpected and many can get quite excited about changes. Whilst it is a good idea to have a settled and reasonably predictable classroom environment, it is also advisable to ring the changes every so often – perhaps changing the seating arrangements and the position of desks.

9 Class norms

Every classroom has routines which are normal for that classroom. This can be beneficial as is indicated above. At the same time, routine can cause some anxiety for new members of the class and for children who have difficulty adjusting to different classrooms particularly in secondary school. It is a good idea to have the classroom rules or habits clearly displayed so that children can refer to them periodically. It is also an idea to develop these rules/habits in conjunction with the children.

10 Structure

All children need a structure but it is important not to over-structure the environment for children. One of the key aims of education is to promote independent thinking – and this can be restricted if the learning environment is too structured.

A classroom environment that is too structured can very easily become teacher-centred. It is important to turn this into a learner-centred environment in order that the structure would have some flexibility to accommodate the needs of learners.

11 Degree of choice

Following on from this it must be remembered that learning environments belong to children. They are the learners and the environment should be tailored to meet their needs. It is important therefore that a degree of choice is provided so the children can select for themselves the kind of environment they want.

12 Informal learning environment

Some learners, and particularly those who find conventional learning challenging, often learn best in an informal learning environment. This means that seating arrangements should be in groups or in any other way than that of conventional rows. Often children who prefer an informal learning environment prefer sitting on the floor or a bean bag. There should be ample space for mobility within the classroom and opportunities for discussion should be available as informal learners often prefer to learn through discussion.

13 Opportunities for exploratory learning

This is very important as quite often classroom environments can be restrictive. It is a good idea to have areas that are designated for problem-solving activities and this could be reflected in the wall displays. It is also important that items in the classroom are easy to locate, especially for new children in a class and for students in secondary school where they may experience a variety of classrooms. Some of the main items that children will need must be easy to locate and this can provide opportunities for exploratory learning.

14 A visually appealing classroom to work in

The effects of a classroom environment can make an impact almost as soon as one goes through the door. This first impression is very important and can often be determined by the visual appeal of a classroom, not only for the children but also for any parents and visitors.

15 Provides students with a sense of ownership and responsibility

There are a number of different ways of doing this. One way is to give groups of students their own space – either a wall space or study space – and get them to organise it the way they wish. It is their responsibility to monitor and change it from time to time. It is crucial that the children see the learning environment as their own and that they feel responsible for it in some way.

16 A stimulating and supportive environment

There are many different factors that can constitute a stimulating environment and an environment that is stimulating for some may not be stimulating for others. As a general rule factors that constitute a stimulating environment include: visually appeal; a degree of choice; space; opportunities for group work and background music. It is important however to contextualise this for particular classes and their preferences. A stimulating environment is also one in which the children feel at home and are motivated to work in a stress-free and constructive manner. The classroom environment should be a source of support for the child which means that in addition to being stress-free it should be resourceful. This would allow a child to use the classroom environment as a place for finding out information and for exploratory work, implying a degree of freedom within the environment for them to work and move around.

17 Stimulate all the senses (VAK)
Learning is always more effective if it is multisensory. That means the learning environment should accommodate visual, auditory and kinaesthetic learning preferences. This can be done through wall displays, tapes and headphones being available for use, and giving the freedom to move around the classroom and explore different learning situations.

18 An atmosphere free of pressure and stress
Irrespective of the type of classroom environment available it is crucial that it is free from stress. Children can be very sensitive to stress in learning situations – many with specific difficulties can find a great deal of learning tasks stressful so it is important that the environment is as stress-free as possible.

19 Allow social interaction for a significant percentage of activities
This is also important and can be even more so for certain types of learners. Space can be a significant consideration when planning activities and this means ensuring that desks are not fixed to the floor and that all the classroom furniture can be moved to accommodate to class activities that may require space.

20 Promote the development of a broad range of skills and interests – intellectual, physical, aesthetic, social and emotional
This can be reflected in wall displays and in the resources available within classrooms. The above categories must be considered. Intellectual – does the classroom stimulate enquiry? Physical – are there opportunities for movement? Aesthetic – is music available and are the wall displays visually appealing? Social – are there opportunities for group work? And finally emotional – is the environment supportive of each child's learning preference? (See also CD Rom Activity 7 on the learning environment – an audit.)

Key Points to Remember

- It is important to ensure that the learning environment is flexible so that it can accommodate the range of learning preferences within a class.
- There should be a sense of ownership within a class and it is vital that children see the classroom environment as their own and that they have some control over how it is organised.
- This applies to all aspects of the environment such as wall displays and the layout of desks and chairs, as well as the degree of movement and the availability of music to listen to whilst working.

The Learning Environment

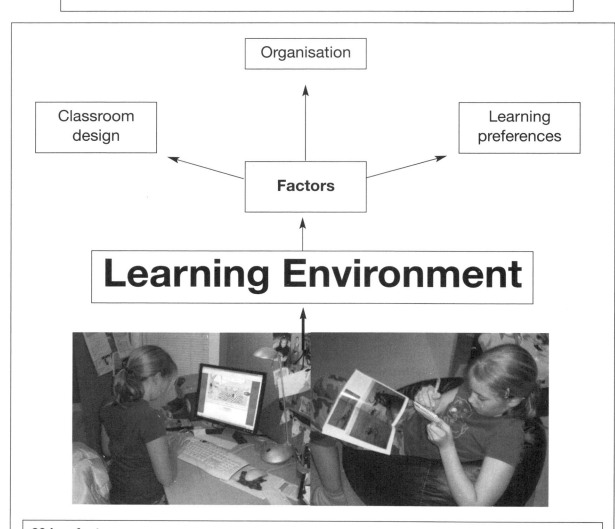

Organisation

Classroom design

Learning preferences

Factors

Learning Environment

20 key factors

1. layout
2. design
3. teacher's base
4. student desks
5. flexibility
6. colour
7. light
8. routine
9. class norms
10. structure
11. choice
12. informal environment
13. opportunities for exploratory learning
14. visually appealing
15. student ownership

16. environment stimulation
17. stimulate senses
18. stress free
19. social interaction
20. encourages personal development

Memory – recognise, revise, review, recall and reflect

This chapter will provide strategies for developing skills in memory. The key to an effective memory is not necessarily gathering a host of strategies – an effective memory depends a great deal on organisation. It is important that learners develop effective organisational strategies to ensure that when they are learning new information it will be understood and retained. To a great extent memory strategies are usually a focus for children further up the school and at college. Much of the strategies in this chapter can be applicable to these groups. At the same time it is important to focus on memory strategies for younger children too and some of the strategies in this chapter can be contextualised for younger children.

The development of effective memory skills has implications for how children take notes and how key points are identified, as well as planning learning and reflection. This chapter will therefore provide:

■ a framework for organisation to enhance memory skills

■ a discussion of different methods of note taking

■ insights into reflection and self-correction

■ a top ten of memory tips.

Setting goals

It is important that realistic goals are set for learners. It is also important that learners are involved in the development of these goals. Quite often a teacher may have to realign expectations because learners are not ready to meet the expectations and goals set by the teacher.

Tips for setting goals

Prioritise

Everyone, including children, has always too many things to do. We are surrounded by choice and decisions every day. It is necessary therefore to prioritise, but for some people that can be difficult and it is necessary to gain practice in doing this. When a student has a list of things to achieve it can be difficult for him /her to decide what to do first and what is less important. This can apply to daily tasks as well as to specific areas of study (such as writing an essay). It is important that children are presented with dilemmas that require decisions to be made and can practise prioritising the different tasks to be carried out. This can be done on a daily task or weekly task basis.

> ## DAILY PRIORITY TASK
>
> Together with the children make a list of all the things they have to carry out in a day, including the evening. Get them to put 1, 2 or 3 after each (with 1 being very important and 3 less important) and then to list all the items. They then must write this list in order of importance.
>
> The same can be done for the weekly list which will be different as it includes weekends.

Prioritising actions can help to clear the mind of competing tasks to be carried out and this will allow students to focus exclusively on the task in hand and not worry about the other things that have to be carried out.

Planning and prioritising

One of the benefits of prioritising when undertaking a task is that it can help with both sequencing and also planning for the various activities that must be carried out. The example below provides guidance on this when preparing to write an essay, by reading through the main text. The idea is that by tackling one aspect at a time you unburden the load on the memory and this can make the task less arduous. (See CD Rom Activity 24 on My Supports and Activity 25 on My Study Plan.)

Postpone

Do not be afraid to postpone things that you feel should be done. This is part of the art of prioritising. If postponing something you should give it a rough timescale – for example, 'next week' or 'after I tackle this ... ' but it is important to note this so you can remind yourself it still has to be done.

Reading the Main Text Priority List

1 Note the key words.

2 List the people or places.

3 Read through the contents and index.

4 Reflect on the overview of the book.

5 Make a rough outline of the book.

6 Read the headings of the chapter to get an overview of the chapter.

7 Read the introductions and summaries.

Action

Goals can only be achieved if they are acted upon. It is important therefore that the goals that you set are achievable and that they can be carried out. It is action not planning that achieves goals, but therefore a realistic and achievable plan must be set.

Monitor

This is significant as monitoring can reassure you that you are on track and can also serve as an aid to memory. It can be helpful when making out a planning sheet to have a column to monitor progress, for example:

47

Monitoring Planning Sheet		
Task	**Progress/Comments**	**Carried out**

Paul Chapman Publishing © Gavin Reid 2007

Praise

One of the most important factors in prioritising is motivation as this can help with achievement which in turn can help to ease the burden on memory as it means there are fewer things to remember to carry out. Two of the key factors are motivation are feedback and praise. It is worthwhile to build feedback into every learning experience and this should highlight the positive. Suggestions for progress should be framed in a constructive way which can be done by first stating what a student has achieved and then going on to discuss how this can be improved. This should be done in the form of a suggestion.

Organisation

As indicated above, one of the reasons why some people have a good memory is because they are able to organise the information at the time of learning and immediately afterwards. Students should practise using a framework for organisation. 💿 (See CD Rom Activity 8 on revision strategy – organisation.)

Framework for organisation
Select

This involves self-questioning to ascertain those areas that are important in a task or a piece of new learning. This involves focusing on only the necessary information.

> **QUESTIONS FOR SELECTION**
>
> Who are the main players or characters in the text?
> How do I know that?
> What is the background to the story or event?
> How were the people feeling?
> What was the background like?
> Were the people happy?
> What was the climate at the time?

Order

This is an important factor in memory work – some people can remember information better if it is sequenced for them. This can be done in history, through the use of a time line that can sequence events, and also when studying a novel. Many children need this type of structure and it is a good way of chunking events together. For example, a task to practise this could be to chunk all the events that have happened in the first chapter of a book (or in the reign of a monarch in history) and to make a list of these.

Children preparing to work independently on an essay also need to impose some order as once again this can reduce memory load.

Ordering tasks for essay writing

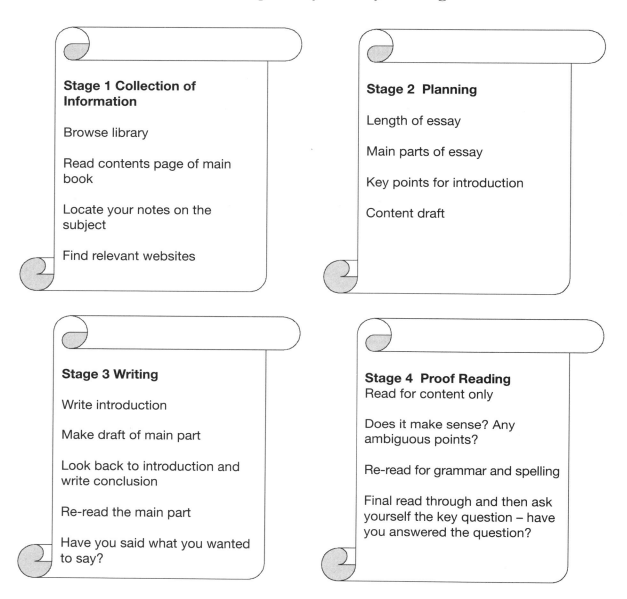

Stage 1 Collection of Information

Browse library

Read contents page of main book

Locate your notes on the subject

Find relevant websites

Stage 2 Planning

Length of essay

Main parts of essay

Key points for introduction

Content draft

Stage 3 Writing

Write introduction

Make draft of main part

Look back to introduction and write conclusion

Re-read the main part

Have you said what you wanted to say?

Stage 4 Proof Reading
Read for content only

Does it make sense? Any ambiguous points?

Re-read for grammar and spelling

Final read through and then ask yourself the key question – have you answered the question?

Note taking

Making notes is an art, yet many children do not get any practice in this and it does require practice. For many children it does not come easily.

KEY POINTS ON NOTE TAKING

Title
This gives you a framework which is necessary for recall.

Listen/read
Do not write straight away – listen if it is a lecture or read if you are taking notes from a book. It is a common mistake to start writing immediately – get the layout of the talk or chapter first and then plan how you are going to write notes.

Do not attempt to write sentences
If you are listening to someone talking it is likely they will be using sentences – it is too easy to try to write down what he/she is saying word for word. This is a mistake as you will be left with a host of unfinished sentences. That is why it is important to listen and write down key words and phrases. Similarly when taking notes from a book do not attempt to copy word by word from a book – read a paragraph and then write down a few phrases on what it means and the implications.

Note facts
Listening to a talk or reading a book can give you a framework of facts. This is important and you should then be in a position to reflect on this information. You may want to write an idea or two on implications as you are writing the information. You can do this in a chart such as the one below.

Reflect immediately afterwards
This is important as it is the whole point of note taking. It provides you with the information to reflect on the issues – the table below can also be useful for that purpose.

Note taking plan

Source	Facts/information	Implications	Importance and why?

Noting facts and information

Five key points to consider here are:

- **Headings** – these are the key to developing concepts and chunking the information. It is also very worthwhile to have a system for using sub-headings.

- **Visuals** – this is also important especially if the learner has a visual learning style. Small drawings sketches or even symbols can all help as memory aids. 💿 (See CD Rom Activity 9 on revision strategy – mind mapping.)

- **Personalisation** – looking at other people's notes may not be too helpful as these need to be personalised and that includes handouts from teachers or lecturers. Students needs to write their own comments on the handout and these comments should be the implications as the handout will likely contain all the necessary facts. So a student can have a heading of 'implications' in the margin, and can write going down the page each implication as a phrase next to the relevant paragraph.

- **Reassignment** – never be afraid to change your mind or to change the order of something – you may find for example that you prefer writing a conclusion to an essay first. It is important to experiment with how you organise yourself and your work.

- **Application** – this really means action – a common mistake is for learners to spend lots of time planning but not being able to carry these plans through. This is because often plans, targets and expectations are too ambitious. Once you have done a plan check how it can be implemented. This is the key to success and successful implementation can be a great stress reducer – and can also unload the burden on the memory.

Top Ten Memory Tips

1 Chunk

Place all similar pieces of information into one group – for example, if you are studying the geography of a country make a chunk of all the facts relating to climate. You should be able to chunk these four items together so find these four (or more) that have a strong connection.

2 Organise

Plan learning and organise your time, your notes and your thoughts – this is the key to an effective memory.

3 Plan

Plan, plan, plan, but remember this does not need to be a linear plan – it could be a mind map or some other symbolic representation.

4 Visualise

It is more effective to use all your senses when learning. This means using the visual modality and for some learners this is very important. Even if you do not feel you are a visual person graphic or a symbol can help to strengthen the memory trace.

5 Connect

You need to make connections all the time when learning. This makes learning meaningful and aids understanding and the development of concepts. An effective learner is one who is able to make these connections. The main connection is between previous learning and new learning. Questions a learner needs to consider are: is there anything about the new learning that is familiar? What is familiar and why? This will help learners to connect between previous and new learning and make the learning more efficient.

6 Imagine

One of the important aspects about memory is that it is very personal. Memory is individual and the more individual it is the more effective retention can be. That is why imagination can be useful. Using imaginative images to make connections can stamp a personal identity on the information to be remembered. So make it personal and make it imaginative – that way the information will be retained more effectively.

7 Repeat

It is unusual to remember information first time around, but rote repetition is not always effective. When repeating information do this in a range of different ways. Use memory cards, visuals, headings, summaries, notes and discussion. All these can be repeating the same information but using various means to do this. This is how information is consolidated and mastered. Mastery is the aim of learning and that will take time and considerable over-learning.

8 Re-enact

Learning should be active. The more active the learner is the more likely the information is understood and retained. This activity could be in the form of discussion but it could also be in drama form and first-person speech. This can be done more easily in some subjects such as history where the first person and drama can be used to re-enact historical events. But these principles can be used across the board in other subjects.

9 Understand

Understanding is vitally important for effective learning and for memory. Take time to ensure the information is understood. You can check understanding by asking yourself questions about the information such as: Why? What? When? How? So What? If you can answer these types of questions then it is likely you have some understanding of the topic. But understanding is vital and without this it will be more difficult to retain information over the long term.

10 Discuss

For some learners discussion is the only way in which they can retain and understand information. Discussion can make the information meaningful and can help a learner experiment with ideas and views. It is this experimentation that helps learners extend their thinking and learning. For some learners discussion can be like thinking aloud.

★ KEY POINT

Understanding is the key to the efficient use of memory. Understanding comes before retention but will make retention easier, particularly over the long term.

Key Points to Remember

This chapter has provided a framework for memory as well as some memory strategies. It is important for an individual to

- **recognise** – to identify his/her own preferred way of learning. Using this preference will ensure that learning and memory will be more efficient. It is also important to plan a programme in order to revise.

- **revise** – the information that is to be learnt. The significant point here is that this revision can take a number of different forms but will work more effectively if there is a revision plan and timetable.

- **review** – the information as it is this reviewing that consolidates memory and ensures understanding and retention in the long-term memory. This will make it easier to bring to mind.

- **recall** – the information but this also needs to be practised. In simple form, the more you use a skill or piece of information the more easily it will be memorised and recalled in future use.

- **reflect** – one of the keys to memory and to understanding is this ability. This can be done through the use of reflective questions such as why and how, but also through thinking (and even thinking aloud).

The key points therefore of this chapter are shown in the summary in bold – recognise, revise, review, recall and reflect. These factors hold the key to an effective memory.

Chapter 5 At a Glance
Memory – Recognise, Revise, Review, Recall and Reflect

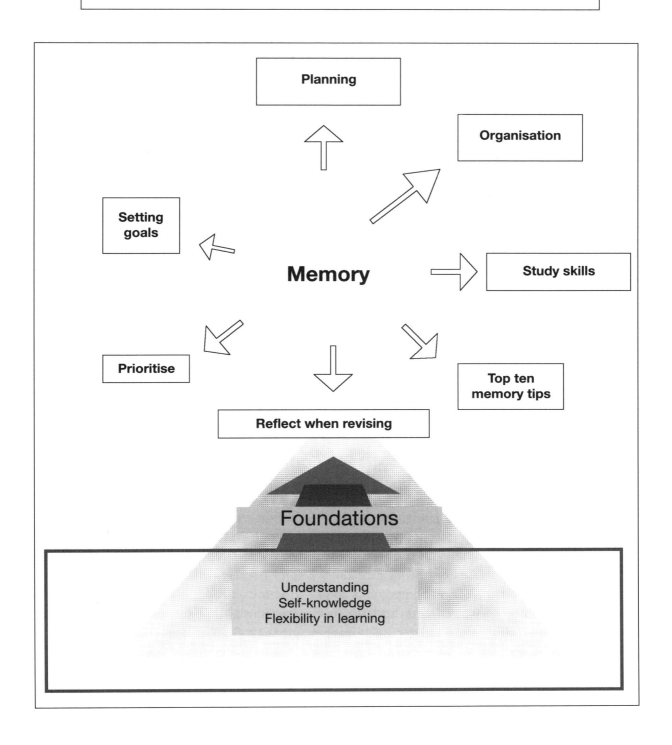

Planning

Organisation

Setting goals

Memory

Study skills

Prioritise

Top ten memory tips

Reflect when revising

Foundations

Understanding
Self-knowledge
Flexibility in learning

Tasks and expectations 6

Learners need to be optimistic – that is the source of motivation and eventual success. At the same time they need to be realistic and set themselves tasks and goals that can be realised. This is an important factor for motivation and effective learning. The actual task that is set and the expectations of how that task can be achieved are crucial for motivation.

This chapter will therefore provide:

- ■ strategies and suggestions on aspects relating to task development and presentation

- ■ a discussion of factors relating to learner expectations such as attitude, self-fulfilment, setting realistic goals and assessing success.

 KEY POINT

DISCUSSING GOALS AND EXPECTATIONS WITH LEARNERS

It is important to discuss goals and expectations with learners. This is crucial as a learner's perception of a task needs to be the same as their teacher's. Learners may see a task as very demanding even though it is well within their abilities. It is important to discuss a task with a learner and as a result the time frame or aspects of the task may need to be re-framed. It is also important to get to know learners. If we reuse the same question on different worksheets, learners' understanding of that same question can be quite different, and for some it could present another challenge from the one that the teacher envisaged. It is worthwhile therefore to engage in pre-task discussion with learners to ensure that both they and the teacher have a common understanding of the task in hand.

Task development

A successful learning outcome starts with the task – and not the learner. It is the task that can determine the outcome. Some of the key factors relating to the development and presentations of tasks are discussed below.

Language

Ideally tasks should contain short sentences. Three short sentences are better than one long one. For learners further up the school who are usually working independently it is important to ensure they have an understanding of what the question means. Understanding what the question actually means or implies can be just as challenging for some learners as the actual answer itself.

Some questions, particularly for learners further up the school, can be phrased in ways that can confuse. For example words like **calculate**, **compare**, **contrast**, **define**, **describe**, **discuss**, **explain**, **justify** *and* **summarise** can all give rise to confusion. Learners can practise using these to ensure they know the distinctions. This can be done as a game activity by providing the following phrases and asking learners to match them with the those above.

The bulleted list below follows the sequence of the words displayed and can be jumbled up to make it a game activity.

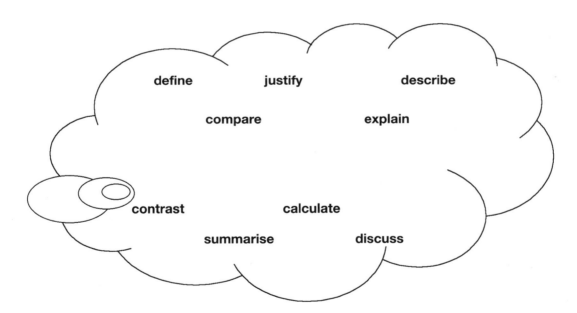

■ finding a numerical answer

■ identifying differences and similarities

■ comparing pieces of information with a focus on the differences

■ giving a precise description or meaning for something

- providing a series of points in sentences that give an overview of the text or event that is being described

- displaying the points for and against a certain point and providing a conclusion at the end

- showing that you understand a particular point, text, or piece of information

- providing a statement as to why something happened or why you have a certain viewpoint

- providing a short account of a text or piece of information that provides the main outline.

Although the previous activities and some of those following are more directed for learners in the 11–18 age range, their principles can be applied to younger learners and contextualised for different aspects of learning for all age groups.

Subject specific vocabulary

For learners further up the school clarification can occur in the use of technical and subject specific vocabulary. For example in biology or in food nutrition the following terms may need clarification.

Absorption = the taking up of a substance.
Amino acid = the smallest unit of protein.
Carbohydrate = food substance that provides energy.
Catalyst = a substance that speeds up a chemical reaction, but doesn't change during the reaction.
Digestion = food is broken down mechanically and chemically so the nutrients can be absorbed.
Enzyme = biological catalyst.
Fat = food that provides energy, but is often stored in the body.
Glucose = the simplest sugar (carbohydrate).
Mineral = chemicals that living things need.
Nutrient = a substance that plants and animals need to live and grow.
Nutrition = food.
Peristalsis = the process of muscles in the oesophagus contracting and relaxing to push food down.
Protein = food substance that is needed for growing and repairing the body.
Vitamin = natural substances that are needed (in small amounts) for growth and health.

Structure

Quite often learning is a sequential experience, with new learning building on previous learning. It is therefore important to consolidate one point before moving on to another. This applies to younger learners as well as those in the 11–18 age range.

For example, this also applies to setting tasks in worksheets. It is good practice to start with a basic task that should not put too many demands on learners. This first question should provide a basis for what is to follow, so ideally it should be a fairly general one. Worksheets therefore need to be structured to make the experience as straightforward as possible for learners. It is also a good idea to use headings and sub-headings throughout worksheets. This can provide a framework as well as a structure as shown in the example below.

Worksheet on Causes of World War 2

Headings and sub-headings

- **Countries involved**
  - Asia
  - Europe
  - America
  - Middle East
- **Politics**
  - Democracies
  - Military regimes
  - Revolutionary governments
- **People**
  - Personalities
  - Background
  - Uniforms
- **Tactics**
  - Air
  - Weapons
  - Battles
- **Blame**
  - Aggressors
  - Defenders
  - Empires
- **Opinions**
  - Press
  - People
  - Nationalities

These headings can provide a structure and each of the sub-headings can also be structured to show headings and sub-headings. This structure is essential for many learners and can help them develop concepts and provide a schema or a framework to help with learning, organisation and recall.

Questions

Ideally it is more effective to encourage learners to self-question. For some learners however this may not be too easy. A framework for self-questioning should be provided. The example shown below can be adapted for all age groups.

FRAMEWORK FOR SELF-QUESTIONING

- What am I being asked to do?
- Why am I being asked to do this?
- How much information do I need to provide?
- Where will I get this information?
- What do I know already about the topic?
- Where did I get this information from?
- Can I go back to these sources?
- How will I know if I am on the right track?
- How long should this task take me?
- What are the different ways of responding to the task?

Reflection

The questions shown above can also be used as the first stage in reflection. It is worth your while to emphasise to learners that education is not a race – whilst examinations are usually timed, learning is not. Learners differ in how long they might take to master a piece of new learning. It is crucial that learners appreciate that being first to complete a task is not necessarily an achievement. I still remember very clearly sitting a final university examination and looking at a fellow student across from me, noting that he was sitting gazing into space and did not seem to be joining in the writing race that preoccupied all the other students in the room. I found out later when I approached the student that he was **reflecting**. That made me rethink my examination style, especially when I found out that that particular student received top marks in the exam!

As a student I had never been taught to reflect – it was assumed one would just do this. But it may not be as simple as it sounds. Some learners do not consider reflection as part of learning.

★ **KEY POINT**

REFLECTION

Reflection is important but can take different forms for different learners. Reflection is very individualised – some people reflect by discussing, others by listening to music, some through exercise and others by thinking alone. It is important to help learners identify their preferred way of reflecting and to support and guide them to use this effectively.

How can you encourage and prepare learners for reflection?

Different learners will likely adopt different styles of reflection and some of these differences will depend on particular learning styles. For example, some may prefer to reflect with the help of background music whilst others will wish for total silence. It is necessary to allow learners to select how they should reflect but this should be an integral part of the learning experience.

The diagram below indicates the main aspects of reflection and an example of the reflection process.

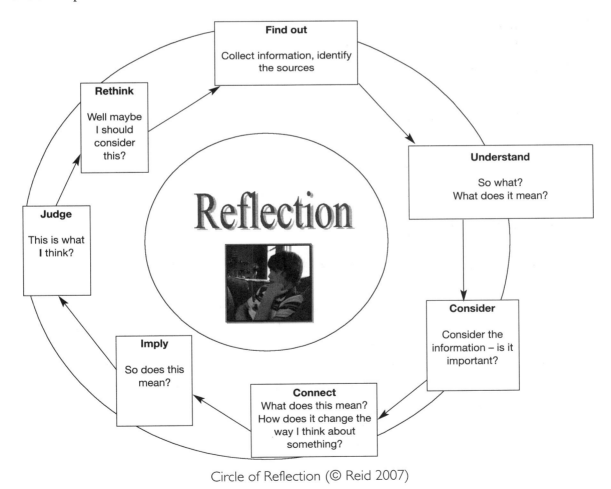

Circle of Reflection (© Reid 2007)

As the figure above shows reflection can be circular and learners can come back to the point where they started and use the reflection to rethink their position on whatever they are learning. Reflection therefore is a learning tool as well as one that can demonstrate a higher level of thinking.

Learning style and task development

Learning styles have already been discussed in Chapter 3 but it is important to consider them in relation to task development. This is shown in the example below.

Learning Style	Task
Auditory	Make lists, find out information
Visual	Make drawings, diagrams, use DVD, computer programs
Kinaesthetic	Arrange visits, activities, field trips
Persistent	Lengthy tasks, problem-solving activities
Global	Provide overview, short tasks, frequent breaks, discussion
Social	Work in groups, in pairs, discussion
Metacognitive	Problem solving, thinking skills
Tactile	Hands-on, model making, demonstration

If the task is quite challenging for learners then it is best if the learning experience focuses heavily on individual learning styles initially. This will help students get into the task more easily and then they can use other modalities. But they will perform better using their own preferred style of learning in the initial stages of learning.

Monitoring

Monitoring is more than checking – it is a bridge between teacher-directed and learner-controlled learning. Ideally the aim should be for students to direct and control their own monitoring of tasks. It is certainly much simpler for a teacher to monitor and check that students are on the right track – this is usually not too time-consuming – but it is possible to turn monitoring into a learning experience by eventually attempting to help students with self-monitoring.

The framework below may provide some guidance for this and shows how a student can take responsibility for their own monitoring. This involves getting them to look at what they want to achieve – the outcome – and to think about what they have already achieved, how they think they should advance and what other materials they might need. It is important that younger learners as well as those in the 11+ age group are introduced to this type of activity. The example below of self-monitoring therefore is not just for older children but should be introduced as early as possible, with all learners encouraged to utilise this type of learning as it promotes learner independence.

Student Self-Monitoring Framework

Outcome	Achievements	Sequence	Plan	Materials
What I want to achieve	What I have done	What I am going to do next	What else do I have to do?	What other resources might I need?

Assessment

One of the key factors to consider about assessment is that it is distinct from testing! A test is a product that looks at the here and now and how a learner performs on a given day with that particular test. This kind of information is important but it is only part of the overall picture of assessment.

Assessment is a process and that process should take place over a period of time ideally with different types of tasks. The idea of assessment is to build up a profile of a student to assist in further teaching and learning. Assessment therefore is a teaching procedure, not a testing one.

It is important that the learner can see the tasks in the assessment as achievable – perhaps not immediately but after some direction and guidance. The idea therefore is to use assessment to help students perform and eventually to achieve all the outcomes in the assessment. The circle of reflection shown earlier in this chapter can also be used a guide to the assessment process.

 **KEY POINT**

ASSESS FOR SUCCESS

Assessment is about assessing success and should identify how students can achieve success. That can involve re-framing the task to ensure students can then understand and succeed with the task. There are a number of means of assessment such as informal assessment through observation, formal assessment through the use of testing, constructive feedback, building on previous achievements, structured reflection, self-monitoring and self-assessment.

As well as encouraging self-monitoring and self-assessment it may be necessary for a teacher also to monitor how students are tackling the task. This is highlighted below.

THE ASSESSMENT PROCESS – TEACHER MONITORING OF TASKS

- Learning outcomes – are they achievable?
- What has the student still to achieve?
- Why have the tasks not been achieved?
- What parts of the task need to be adapted to obtain success?
- How will this help a student to move on to other tasks?
- What materials/supports may a student still require?

Expectations

Setting realistic goals

Setting realistic goals and reaching these goals are all about noting the achievements that have been made and being aware of what needs to be done to develop these achievements to meet the goals. Often learners set their sights too high and ignore what they have already achieved even if they have not fully reached their target goal. It is necessary for learners to realise that reaching goals is a process and one which they can have a great deal of control over. If they focus too much on achieving the goals that are set they may become overwhelmed because the goals may represent too big a leap. That is why they need to record achievements. It is from this that the goals can become realistic and achievable. The key point is therefore to ensure that achievements have been noted even if these seem very minor compared to the overall goal. This is shown below.

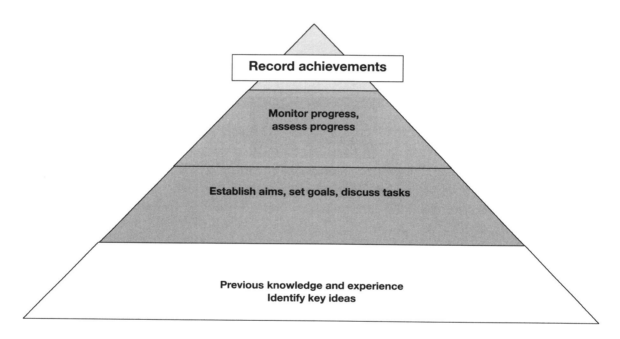

Previous experience

Goals and achievements need to be built up from a foundation of experience. Previous knowledge is therefore very important but this has to be utilised effectively. Some learners have significant difficulties in accessing their previous knowledge and understanding and using this for new learning.

Using previous knowledge

A framework can be developed for this, such as that shown opposite.

Previous Knowledge

Vocabulary

Words I know   Words I do not know

Information

What I know   Still to find out

Background

What do I already know about this?   What areas do I have little knowledge in?

Resources

Resources I still need   Where these are to be found

The above can be developed depending on the subject area. For example, in history there can be a column for people, in geography this could be for features of a country. It is best to make up a list of headings on the topic and present these to students. For example, in science if students are learning about electricity you can use words like energy, force, machines, sound, light and radioactivity.

What is realistic?

What is realistic depends on the individual learner – that is why it is important to get to know them when developing tasks – plus their strengths and weaknesses and their learning preference, as well as any background understanding they have on the topic.

Other important aspects to consider in developing realistic tasks include:

- the steps and the sequence and how clearly they are provided for a learner

- a learner's experience of the topic and the type of learning they will be involved in

- the skills a learner has in self-monitoring and being able to gauge whether they are on the right track or not.

Goal setting

It is important however to set learners goals that they have to strive to achieve. If a goal is too easy it may belittle the achievement and may not stimulate learners. Goals must be realistic but at the same time they must be challenging. It is this balance between what is realistic and what is challenging that places demands on teachers.

Feedback

In order for learners to maintain motivation it is important that feedback is provided throughout a task as well as at the end of the task. Feedback should offer:

- **Guidance:** the key point of any feedback is to provide learners with guidance to ensure that they are progressing towards achieving the task. Guidance can and should be framed in a positive way.

- **Positive reinforcement:** it is vital to start with positive comments and then some points for development can be mentioned – it is important that positive comments are made both initially and at the end of any feedback session.

- **Assessment of progress:** ideally this should be done by a learner and the key point of this is to attempt to empower them sufficiently so that he/she can take on the responsibility of self-monitoring their own work. This highlights the need for learners to gain some control over their own learning.

- **Suggestions for further work:** it is also important that learners are left with a framework and suggestions for development. Further reading, additional resources that can be accessed and other points that can be made are all important.

■ **Opportunities to develop self-monitoring and self-assessment:** essentially this is what feedback is all about – empowering a learner to take control over his/her own learning. Constructive teacher feedback framed in a positive tone can help a learner to achieve this.

Success

This chapter is about tasks and expectations. Irrespective of the task and the expectation it is crucial that learners can perceive and experience success. Learners' perceptions of success are important and this is applicable to children of all ages. It is worth also bearing in mind that success for a learner may be different to their teacher's view of success. It is important that time is taken at the start of a task to ensure that these perceptions can match. A learner has to be sure of what they are trying to achieve and it is the teacher's role to ensure that this clarity and a common and achievable goal are evident. It is surprising how many learners can actually achieve the goals of a task and still think they have not done well. In this type of situation questions need to be asked about the pre-task discussion and whether or not there is a shared goal and shared expectations of the task.

A point made earlier in this book is that success is necessary for success. All the points mentioned in this chapter reiterate this statement and the strategies promoted here are geared towards that end.

Key Points to Remember

This chapter has

■ Examined some key aspects of task development.

■ Highlighted the importance of the type of language used in tasks.

■ Emphasised the need to structure tasks and to build a framework for tasks based on learners' experiences and previous knowledge.

■ Strongly suggested that student reflection is important for successful outcomes and every opportunity should be made within a task for this to occur.

■ Indicated that the development of all tasks needs to start from a knowledge base of a learner's style and learning preference.

■ Also indicated that the teacher and the student must have a common appreciation of the task and a shared expectation of what represents a successful outcome. It is this common expectation that is important and this can determine the extent of differentiation and adaptation that is needed when developing a task.

Tasks and Expectations

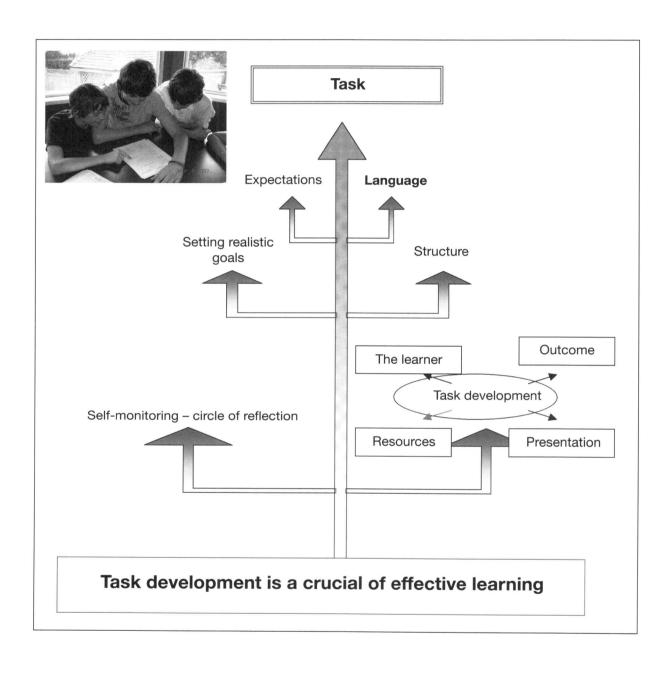

Task

Expectations   **Language**

Setting realistic goals

Structure

The learner

Outcome

Task development

Self-monitoring – circle of reflection

Resources

Presentation

Task development is a crucial of effective learning

Social and emotional factors 7

This chapter will look at some key social and emotional aspects of learning. The chapter will focus on

■ the feelings people experience when learning

■ the role and importance of social and emotional development on learning

■ the impact of stress on learning and the learning environment.

Social learning

Learning can be fun and in order for it to be effective it should be! Some learners however find the idea of learning in isolation quite traumatic and de-motivating and many learners need to be involved socially when they learn. This involves working in groups, or being able to collaborate with at least one other person.

Examples of social learning

■ **Group tasks**
  Any task that involves small groups can facilitate social learning – it is important to ensure that the progress made in groups is closely monitored

■ **Paired learning**
  This is two children learning at the same time. It can be in the form of a structured activity such as paired reading, paired spelling or paired thinking, or unstructured activities involving two children learning together.

- **Classroom activities**

  Some classroom activities such as Circle Time can be very useful in developing social learning. These activities can promote turn taking, positive attitudes, awareness of the needs of others and the development of a positive self-concept.

- **Discussion**

  This can be an excellent tool for developing social learning but it is important that all children are able to participate in the discussion – it may be helpful to provide discussion sheets to guide this and to give a role to each member of the group.

- **Drama**

  Drama is an excellent example of social learning. Again it is important that all children have a role as it can be demoralising if any child feels left out. It is worthwhile to introduce this type of activity as early on as possible and to integrate it into every curriculum area.

- **Poetry writing and reading**

  This can be an excellent way of developing self-esteem and also useful for children with reading difficulties, as poetry can rely more on imagery than prose. Often children with reading difficulties can write poetry quite well. Poetry reading can also be done in groups and this can be both fun and an excellent socialising activity.

- **Role play**

  Most areas of the curriculum can be conducive to role play. History is an obvious example but it can be used in other subjects as well. The key point about role play is that it should allow a child to improvise. This is excellent for those children who may not be able to remember scripts or detailed information but have a good imagination and can improvise well.

- **Team games**

  Team games provide another obvious example of social learning but again it is important to ensure that all children have a role to play in the team and this will involve some pre-planning to structure the activity and close monitoring throughout.

- **Songs/recitals**

  Even those children who cannot sing can find this entertaining and stimulating. Making up songs and performing them can provide a real boost to motivation and the involvement of all in the learning task.

- **Field work**

  Field work is a good example of collaboration – if there is little collaboration then it is likely the field activity will not be successful. It helps children to appreciate the role of others and of the importance of collaboration.

- **Surveys and interviews**

  This can be good for the metacognitive learner. It involves problem solving and then working in small teams and it can be used also as a team building activity, with a competitive edge introduced into it. Those readers who are familiar with the television show *The Apprentice* (which provides tasks for groups in a highly competitive situation with rewards and punishments for winners and losers), can appreciate that many intelligent adults lack the skills to work in teams in a collaborative and positive fashion. It is important that practice in this type of activity is provided at school.

Gains	Dangers
Group tasks	**Group tasks**
■ Team building	■ Child being left out
■ Interaction	■ Uncertainty and hesitancy
■ Motivation	
Paired learning	**Paired learning**
■ Companionship when learning	■ Confusion
■ Security	■ One person taking the lead all the time
■ Confidence	
Classroom activities	**Classroom activities**
■ Feeling included	■ Being excluded
■ Fun	■ Unable to follow task
■ Become familiar with all children in class and not only one or two	■ Not being able to share in any successful outcomes
Discussion	**Discussion**
■ Stimulates thinking	■ May be left out
■ Opportunity to express opinions	■ May not understand topic or task
■ Can help reflection and sharing other viewpoints	■ Can be de-skilling
Drama	**Drama**
■ Develops imagination	■ Can be embarrassing
■ Gets rid of inhibitions	■ May feel left out
■ Good for team building	■ May compare oneself unfavourably with others
■ Can develop understanding of topic	
Poetry reading and writing	**Poetry reading and writing**
■ Can be good for developing imagination	■ May be challenging for some learners
■ Can be fun	■ May not want or be able to read aloud
■ Uses literacy skills based more on imagery and this can be good for some children	

Role play
- Does not rely on certain level of literacy skills
- Can help enhance understanding of topic

Role play
- May be awkward for some children
- May not have had sufficient practice in this type of activity

Team games
- Can be good at team building and boosting self-confidence
- Helps some children fit in with the group/school
- Can boost self-esteem

Team games
- Some children may not fit in
- Some can feel left out
- May feel responsible if letting team down

Songs and recitals
- Can be fun
- Can develop imagination
- Can be multi-sensory
- Can help to develop creativity

Songs and recitals
- Some children may have difficulty in remembering words
- May feel embarrassed about singing

Field work
- Can help to develop thinking skills
- Can help with team building and task sharing

Field work
- For some children the instructions will need to be clearly structured
- May not do the task they are best suited for

All of the above can in some way involve social learning and some learners will only progress if they are given the opportunity to participate in this type of learning. (See also CD Rom Activity 11 on social learning.)

Principles for developing social learning

It is important to acknowledge that some learners will find social learning quite challenging as it involves accommodating, and at times accepting, other learners' ideas and learning habits.

Social learning should therefore be introduced with some care. An important principle to start with is the need to find out what learners' social learning preferences are. An example of how this can be done is shown below and in the CD Rom with this book.

Finding out learners' social learning preferences

This can be done through a learning styles questionnaire. For example:

1   Do you prefer working on your own/ with others?

2   Do you like being part of a team?

3   If you had a difficult learning problem to solve would you

i) talk to one other person?

ii) solve it yourself?

iii) discuss it with a group?

You can also get students to rate the different type of activities that they enjoy doing and from those responses it should be quite clear if they are social learners or not.

Interpreting social learning preferences

Questions and observations on social learning can be interpreted qualitatively. This should provide some insights that can help you at least work out a learner's readiness and preferences for social learning. If a learner comes out with a strong preference for working alone then social learning will need to be introduced carefully. The best way to do this is to begin with the learner working with one other person on a task that he/she is very familiar with and to then progress from there to larger groups. If a learner is put in the midst of a group and is not prepared for this he/she will not get much from the group activity and may well become de-motivated and disaffected.

If a student is new to the school or to your class it is a good idea to pair him or her with someone who is comfortable in a social learning situation – ideally a student who is able to communicate, listen, reflect and question. Students who can work effectively in groups can be excellent at helping students new to the class to settle and feel comfortable in their new situation.

Emotional factors in learning

■ **Feeling good**

This is important as a learner has to want to learn and needs to feel good within him/herself. It is worthwhile taking time to ensure a learner is emotionally ready for the task. Some children (and adults) can feel totally swamped and overwhelmed and it is necessary to talk this through with them before they proceed. Try the Double F, P and R Formula.

■ **At ease with the environment**

Learners have to feel comfortable in the environment and this may not be too obvious. Some learners have little awareness of the best environment for them to learn effectively. This is not surprising since children at school usually have very little choice over their learning environment. It is important therefore to give students some options regarding this, including wall displays, colours, the organisation of desks, seating arrangements and scope for movement, as well as the level of activity and the opportunity for group learning.

■ **Able to access the learning materials**

Inability to access the learning materials could be the reason why some learners stumble emotionally when learning – perhaps the books and other materials they need are beyond their current level of knowledge and understanding. This needs to be checked out with learners.

Double F, P and R Formula

Feelings

- ask how they feel about doing the task

Feedback

- feedback to them what they have already achieved towards doing the task

Perspective

- put in perspective what they have to achieve

Process

- together with the learner talk the process through and indicate clearly what has to be done in order

Reasons

- identify the reasons for any feelings of being overwhelmed and why this should be the case

Realign

- this is about goals and expectations so realign jointly with the learners some suggested goals that can be achieved

Ascertaining readiness

Pre-task

- Identify the key points of the topic.
- Discuss these one by one with the student.
- Ascertain the level of knowledge on each of the key points.
- Identify those points that are new or unknown to the learner.
- Discuss those before embarking on the task.

During the task

- Ask the student if he/she is on target.
- Do they need any further explanation?

■ Do they need any further resources?

■ What else do they need to complete the task?

■ What are the next steps?

At the end of the task

■ Do they think they were successful?

■ What did they find easy/difficult?

■ What could/should they have known before they started the task?

(This last question is important as it relates to how prepared they were for the task.)

Time of day

This is also a key factor in students' emotional preparedness for learning. Some learners may be morning, afternoon or evening learners and this can make a difference to how they feel about a task.

This can be ascertained by asking learners to imagine they have a really difficult task to tackle and if they had a free choice on when to do this task what time of day would they select? Some learners may not have thought about this and may require some prompting to help them become aware that they do have a time of day preference.

Knowledge of subject and task

There can be a number of reasons why a learner is emotionally unprepared for undertaking a task. These include the knowledge base and background understanding needed. This can be checked out as illustrated above (see ascertaining readiness) and ensuring a learner has the background understanding for a task, as this in itself can provide considerable emotional confidence.

 KEY POINT

Understanding is one of the key factors in developing emotional security in learning. If students do not have the background understanding then they will not be prepared for the challenges of a task. Time spent at the beginning to ensure that students have a basic understanding and the necessary background knowledge will pay dividends.

Preparing for learning – developing emotions

Emotional development is important for the process of learning and the eventual success of a task. It is worthwhile spending class time on developing emotional security and helping children to become aware of the emotional side of learning, including how they feel about doing a certain task and why they feel like that. The development of emotions can be seen at three levels: the cognitive (that is how people think); the physiological (that is the current state of bodily health and wellbeing); and the affective domain (which relates to understanding and awareness of one's own and other people's emotions).

Emotional literacy and emotional intelligence

Emotional literacy is essentially being literate, namely being aware of one's emotions and the feelings of others. According to Killick (2005: 14) emotional literacy provides 'a way of increasing the space that exists between feelings and actions'. He argues this can be linked to emotional intelligence. Both relate to the capacity in individuals (and groups) to perceive, understand and manage emotions in oneself and relating to others. This is very important for social learning.

Emotional literacy therefore in order to have any real impact on the education and lives of children has to be fully absorbed and included into a whole-school ethos. Killick suggests that 'emotionally literate children will have greater resilience to emotional problems' (2005: 5) and it is often the case that emotional problems often underlie the behaviour problems that are seen in the classroom.

There are five pathways to emotional intelligence: self-awareness, self-regulation, motivation, empathy and social competence. These are all necessary for the development of emotional wellbeing and emotional literacy.

To ensure that schools have an ethos that is conducive to emotional literacy, factors such as organisational climate, organisational change, bullying, teacher stress, Circle Time communication, motivation, feedback, thinking skills, developing interpersonal skills and the role of reflection are all crucial and most of these factors are included here. Effective learning therefore may well be synonymous with the finer points of emotional literacy.

The cognitive – developing a cognitive skills checklist

- ■ Are the materials at the right reading age level?

- ■ Does the learner have the necessary background knowledge?

- ■ Are there any ideas and concepts that have to be explained?

- ■ Is the task clear?

- ■ Does the learner have sufficient time to complete the task?

- ■ Does the learner have all the necessary resources for the task?

- ■ Is the learner aware of what has to be achieved?

The physiological – a physiological readiness checklist

- Are the lighting and temperature suitable for the learner?

- Is there drinking water available?

- Is the learner happy with the seating arrangements?

- Is the environment at the right noise level for the learner?

Emotional literacy – an emotional literacy preparedness checklist

- Does the learner show any signs of stress?

- Can the student be left to work independently?

- Can the student persist with the task or will he/she require monitoring?

- Can the learner only work for short periods?

- Does the learner require constant reassurance?

- Is the learner aware of the needs of others?

The above can serve as a monitoring or checking sheet to ascertain that a learner is emotionally ready for the task. It may be necessary to do some preparatory work on a learner's emotional wellbeing before they can work independently. It is also worth noting as indicated earlier that emotional literacy is a whole-school responsibility. Children may well develop emotional literacy in one class but if they are in a school which does not have an emotional literacy ethos then any gains will be lost.

Stress and learning

There is a wide range of reasons why learners can experience stress. This includes:

- **State of mind:**
  Some children are more prone and more vulnerable to stress than others. Trigger factors that can result in stress therefore can be different in different children.

- **Worry/anxiety:**
  It is important to be aware that children can worry about things that seem to us as adults to be irrelevant. It is important to take all children's anxieties seriously.

- **Social reasons:**
  School is a social institution but some children find it difficult to fit in. This can make them socially isolated and can be a chronic source of unhappiness for many children.

■ **Family reasons:**

Families and carers occupy a central role in children's lives. If things go wrong or changes are made to family life in whatever way this can have an upsetting effect on some children. Much depends on how the change is handled and the quality and nature of the relationships they have with their parents or carers.

■ **School learning:**

School can also be a competitive institution. This is fine as it can stretch children to achieve but at the same time it can demoralise those who have difficulty in doing so.

■ **School friendships:**

Peer-group friendships are vitally important to most children and a breakdown in these can be the main source of unhappiness at school for some children. This should not be taken lightly and activities such as Circle Time can help to develop peer-group friendships and understanding.

■ **Bullying:**

There has been much written about bullying and many sources of support exist – for example, anti-bullying networks. Some can be found at the following websites (from such different countries as the USA, New Zealand, Australia, the UK, Japan and Canada). www.dfes.gov.uk/bullying/; www.nobully.org.nz/guidelines.htm;www.aic.gov.au/publications/tandi2/tandi259.pdf;www.cops.usdoj.gov/pdf/e12011405.pdf

Bullying is an international phenomenon and every country has taken measures to ensure it does not affect the learning experiences and opportunities of students.

For example, in Japan the schools in Osaka implemented an 'empowerment' programme to fight bullying in 920 public elementary and junior high schools, helping children to develop skills to protect themselves from violence and bullying. The scheme is under the 'Children's Empowerment Support Guidance' programme and students participate in games and role-playing activities based on the idea of empowerment.

The programme works on four areas: sense of belonging, boundaries, emotions and power. In the boundaries component, for example, students gather in pairs and are made aware through games and other activities that the other person has physical and mental boundaries that they must not cross. The students are given tips on preventing violence using a variety of techniques, such as telling the other person they don't like something or looking the other person straight in the eye. In the emotions section, the students are taught techniques to control their anger and to avoid it exploding into violence, such as a breathing exercise using the mental image of a flower blooming.

The programme also includes methods to prevent bullying, such as encouraging students to find their own and other classmates' good points and differences to make them realise that each person is special (see *Mainichi Daily News*, Japan, 25 November 2006, available at mdn.mainichi-msn.co.jp/national/news/20061125p2a00m0na019000c.html).

Another example comes from a local youth theatre group in Guelph, Ontario, Canada. In December 2006 an educational theatre company staged a public performance of a play about bullying entitled 'I Met a Bully On the Hill' aimed at schoolchildren aged 6–13. The play follows the story of an eight year-old girl who moves from the country to the city and goes to a new school where she encounters the school bully. The key theme of the play is to get children to understand the issues surrounding the impact of bullying and to bring these issues into the wider community (available in the *Guelph Tribune*, Ontario, Canada, 24 November 2006).

Bullying is by far the most prevalent cause of emotional insecurity and unhappiness at school. Alarmingly it affects many more children that we often realise.

■ **Unrealistic expectations:**
This is often the main cause of failure in school. It is important that the expectations both from the children's and from their teacher's viewpoint are seen to be flexible. The key aspect to managing expectations relates to ensuring tasks are differentiated sufficiently to ensure that students meet with success. This is discussed in detail in Chapter 6.

Dealing with stress

 **(See also CD Rom Activity 18)**

Individual approaches

■ **Activity:**
Most types of activities can help to alleviate stress. Children often feel more relaxed after exercise as long as it is not of a competitive nature or too prolonged, otherwise it can result in additional stress and fatigue.

The picture above provides an example of unstructured free play and it is important that the play environment is sufficiently safe and resourceful to promote free play in this way. This is where many children are able to express their emotions as well as free themselves of any stresses that may arise from the learning situation.

- ■ **Sport:**

  This is a great stress reliever – it can also help to develop team building and peer friendships.

- ■ **Music:**

  It is important that the right type of music is selected – the best idea is to get a student to try to work and study with different types of music. That way they can work out which, if any, is best for them.

- ■ **Yoga:**

  Yoga involves both mental and physical capacities and can have a relaxing effect on people as it helps them to switch off from their daily routine. This is important for effective learning.

- ■ **Reflection:**

  Reflection essentially means that children need to take time out from what they are doing to reflect. This is vital and therefore must be done. Reflection can help them become aware of where they have been, where they are at and where they want to go. Often the pace of life in school is fast and furious with cramped syllabuses and high expectations. It is important therefore to allow time for reflection. School assemblies can also be used to promote reflection.

- ■ **Talking:**

  Talking through a problem or a situation can help to clarify it in one's mind. This should not be overlooked – it is important to give children the opportunity to do this. Some may not be aware of the nature of the problem until they have actually started to articulate it.

- ■ **Sleep/rest:**

  For many children school life is hectic. The pace is fast and it can be exhausting. It is important to allow time for rest and of course sleep. The source of many periods of unhappiness and misery can in fact be due to lack of rest and can be easily remedied.

- ■ **Reading:**

  Reading can be relaxing but some children have difficulty with this and for them it can be a stressful activity. It is important to try to engage all children in reading and to do this it is crucial that the right level of reading materials is found (this applies to content as well as vocabulary). Many publishers now have a series of high-low books that have a high interest content but a lower level of vocabulary for reluctant readers.

■ **Succeeding:**

Success can be enjoyed and can take much pressure off an individual, but children may not be successful in every area of their school life. It is important therefore that the expectations and the task are both geared to the individual – that way there will be a greater possibility of that person achieving success. To obtain success the task should consider four factors:

a) learner understanding

b) learner control

c) should be achievable

d) should promote learner autonomy.

■ **Hobbies:**

There is certainly more emphasis in school on the development of interests and hobbies. The internet also makes information on these aspects more accessible. This is significant as hobbies cannot only promote the social competences that children need but can also be a useful learning tool. This can help in the transfer of learning from one situation to another – a factor that is crucial for effective learning and one that many learners have some difficulty in recognising.

Group approaches – friendships

Friendships for most children can be the most important ingredient in school life. This needs to be recognised as a breakdown in these friendships can often be at the root of many of the learning, social, emotional and behavioural difficulties seen in schools today.

Systems approaches

Relieving stress is not the responsibility of the individual alone. Many argue that if stress reduction is to have any lasting and far reaching effect a systems approach needs to be considered (see Reid and Hinton 1999 [1996]). Some of the key factors in this approach are shown below.

- **Staff development:**
  Just as in the case of emotional literacy, stress management should be seen as a whole-school initiative. It is only if the school staff collaborate and work together to both identify and deal with the stressors that the school will become teacher and student friendly and as stress free as possible. (Some suggestions for a stress management programme, taking a whole-school approach, are shown on the CD Rom See Activity 18 (Personal Stress Audit), Activity 15 (Stress proofing the school) and Activity 16 (Stress proofing the teacher).)

- **Role clarity:**
  This mainly affects staff and relates to the multi-faceted dimensions of teachers' roles in schools today. These can incur both role ambiguity and role conflict (Reid and Hinton 1999). Often teachers may not be sure of their role and several aspects of it – for example, the conflict that often exists between dealing with the learning and emotional needs of children on the one hand and the need to get through a crowded syllabus and to ensure that students are equipped for examinations on the other hand. Often if any conflict arises it can usually be due to misunderstandings and (very commonly) the inability to identify the actual problem. The problem trigger may not be the same as the problem cause. For example, the trigger can be the behaviour of some children in class but the cause could be that the management have not allowed sufficient planning time to ensure that materials for all the children in class are prepared. One of the first questions therefore to ask is – what exactly is the problem? Only when the problem has been defined can something be done to deal with it.

- **Support:**
  For any classroom, or indeed school, to be a stress-free environment it is important that there is some commitment from the school management. Supports can be in the form of individual stress management sessions, discussions on how the school can be free from institutionalised stress and how to prevent pupil stress through stress prevention and stress alleviation programmes. (Some examples of this and accompanying activities can be found in the CD accompanying this book.)

- **Value:**
  One of the factors that can determine an emotionally healthy school is that staff are valued. If the contribution of staff is valued then it is likely that morale will be

higher, any stress can be dealt with more effectively and in a positive and constructive way and the children themselves are likely to be aware of this so that they themselves will feel more valued.

■ **Ethos:**
The ethos of any school can almost instantly be recognised by visitors – there is something on entering a school that conveys an immediate message on its ethos. Visitors can see this in wall displays and in the motivation of its pupils. The school ethos can therefore be related to how a school and its staff manage their own and others' stress.

■ **Spiritual wellbeing:**
This can also be related to school ethos – essentially a healthy school should cater for the learning, social, emotional and spiritual needs of all within. There can be an overlap between each of these.

Key Points to Remember

- Opportunities should be provided to help all learners develop social learning.
- How one feels at the time of learning is crucial to the outcome.
- It is important to aspire to whole-school initiatives on emotional literacy and stress prevention.
- All the students and teachers in a school need to be valued as this will influence the school ethos and the learning performance of all students.

Social and Emotional Factors

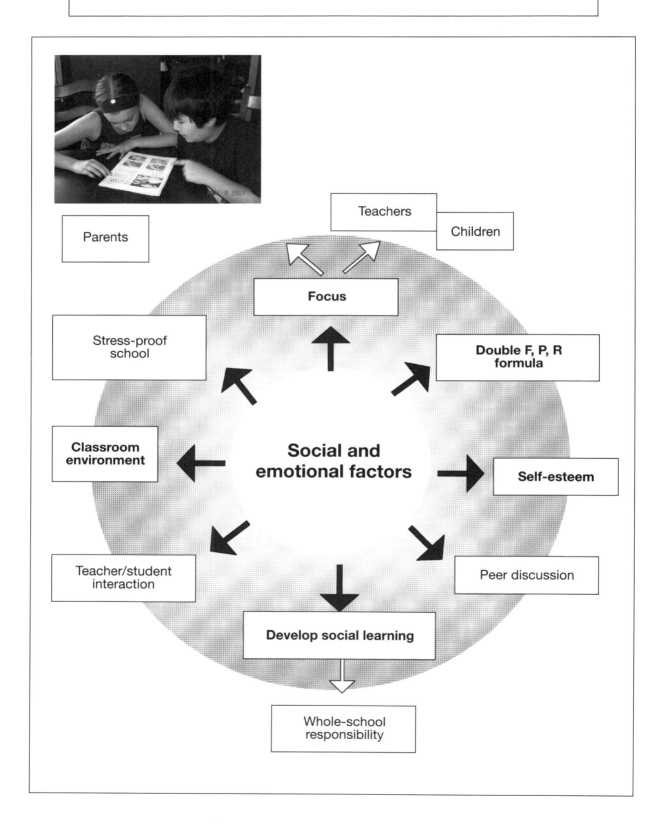

Parents

Teachers

Children

Focus

Stress-proof school

Double F, P, R formula

Classroom environment

Social and emotional factors

Self-esteem

Teacher/student interaction

Peer discussion

Develop social learning

Whole-school responsibility

Managing learning

This chapter will:

- identify 20 key principles of classroom management

- discuss planning and show how to anticipate potential problems

- discuss the need to be proactive

- provide an observational framework and suggestions for motivation

- show how to develop student independence

- discuss issues relating to behaviour management and classroom control

- provide strategies to deal with these as well as supporting children with additional and special needs.

Classroom management

Key principles

Although it is appreciated that no two classroom situations are the same some key principles of effective classroom management can be identified. It is important to acknowledge these principles as they can provide a guide to classroom teaching and learning. (See CD Rom activity 12 – Classroom management.)

Top 20 key principles for classroom management

- **Work with, not against, the students**

   It is crucial that students see you as a supportive source and not a restrictive one. Students need to be sure that you understand their views and you are trying to accommodate those views. There are occasions when it is not possible to follow a student line, especially if it would cause disruption to others, but even in these situations you can still work together with the students to try to arrive at a solution that can be acceptable to all. It is important not to put a student in a position where he/she has to back down and perhaps lose face in front of others.

■ **Acknowledge all efforts**

Rewards and positive feedback need to be provided for all effort – you reward not the achievement but the effort. For many that is an achievement in itself.

■ **Take time to provide individual feedback**

It is important to personalise learning. Feedback needs to be provided on an individual basis with opportunities for students to discuss this. Feedback is an integral part of learning and should be seen not as the final stage in learning but as a source of support, a guide to monitoring and a bridge to achieving the desired learning outcome.

■ **Cater for all, but respect the individual**

In the classroom situation when there is a diversity of needs to be met it is all too easy to forget about the individual while there might be a preoccupation to cater for all. This is a tricky balance to achieve but the key to achieving this is planning. At the planning stage extended work as well as differentiated work for students who need more time should be developed. It is important to know the students you are planning for and this can be done through observation at the pre-planning stage. It is a good idea to develop a framework for doing this so that at least you have an idea of the strengths, weaknesses and learning preferences of the individual students.

■ **Plan, plan, plan**

As suggested above, the key to successful classroom management is planning – this means anticipating the difficulties students can experience in order to prevent failure. Classroom management difficulties can often arise when the task is not demanding and the student is uncertain about how to approach it. Planning should include the materials, a previous knowledge of the students, the process of finding out – the learning part and the proposed outcomes – and the assessment. It is a good idea to develop a checklist for planning such as the one below.

Planning checklist

Area of learning	Materials	Comments
For example, background understanding	For example, need to check the books they have used	For example, need to introduce the topic with key points from the background

Some considerations after the initial planning are shown below.

- Do the activities match the learning objective?

- Is there variety in the types of activities?

- What is the purpose of the groupings used?

- Are the pace and timing right?

- What is the balance between teacher activity and student activity?

- How do you scaffold learning throughout the lesson?

- What type of supports does the learner need?

- What additional resources do you need?

- What provision have you made for the most able/least able in terms of differentiation and in the assessment of the learning outcomes?

- **Anticipate potential problems**
  This emphasises the importance of knowing the students. If for example any of them have a diagnosis of a specific difficulty such as dyslexia, dyspraxia or attention difficulties, then so much is known about these conditions that it should be possible to plan to anticipate the types of challenges these students will encounter. An example is shown below for three well-known syndromes which can be seen in virtually every classroom in every school.

Dyslexia	Dyspraxia	Attention Difficulties
Speed of processing Memory Literacy difficulties Recording information Organisation Self-esteem	Speed of processing Memory Literacy – handwriting Recording information Organisation Self-esteem	Focusing on detail Memory Literacy Accurately recording information Organisation Self-esteem

(with permission, Fil Came, Learning Works Int)

The table above describes the characteristics of three well-known conditions and it can be noted at a glance how these can overlap. There are two key reasons why planning for learning in this way can be useful. Firstly, it is possible to prevent failure from occurring by anticipating these potential challenges and ensuring the students who have these difficulties are not placed in a position where they have to deal with new learning relating to these. For example, if we know a particular student will have difficulty with the speed for processing difficulties then we need to allow more time for that student to complete the task. This should be recognised at the planning stage and this applies to all the characteristics mentioned in the table above.

Secondly, one of the other reasons for planning a table such as the one above is that it allows teachers to note that there can be a significant overlap between these conditions. This has been recognised in the literature (Norwich and Lewis 2001; Reid 2005) which shows that often effective differentiation, supportive literacy intervention and recognition of students' learning preferences are what are required rather than any specialist intervention. The point about overlap is followed up later in this chapter on the teaching and learning process (see page 101).

■ **Gain insights into the learning preferences of the class**
This can be done through observation and it is a good idea to develop a framework for this. An example of this is shown below.

An observational framework

■ Attention

■ Organisation

■ Social skills

■ Learning modality preferences

■ Independent learning

■ Writing skills

■ Number skills.

For each heading in this framework some key aspects can be included depending on the purpose of the observation (see CD Rom Activity 5).

■ **Consult with other staff**
It is important to appreciate that managing behaviour is not one single teacher's responsibility. It is a whole-school concern and a school's policies, processes and school ethos are as instrumental in managing learning as the specific actions a class teacher can take. It is important that an atmosphere of consultation takes place in school so that staff will not feel in any way threatened or undermined by discussing potential and real difficulties with others in the staff. Consultation, collaboration and co-operation should be the key factors in managing learning and staff should see this as a team responsibility.

■ **Remember names**
This may seem quite obvious but in some situations it can be difficult to remember names. It does however make a big difference to mention a student by name when you are working with him/her. This can certainly be difficult in larger secondary and high schools where a teacher may see hundreds of students every week. It is best however to try to develop a seating plan or a working group plan to help remember names.

■ **Provide a balance between student choice and teacher direction**

Ideally students should manage their own learning. This is what we as teachers need to strive for. The emphasis should be on students taking control over their own learning, with teachers relinquishing this responsibility as early in the learning process as possible. This can be a gradual process so that is why there needs to be this balance between student choice and teacher direction to begin with.

■ **Make students feel important and influential in the organisation of the class**

Students need to feel a sense of ownership in the classroom. They should therefore be consulted in the planning of the classroom and in the daily class routine. It is this consultation and consideration that can make them feel it is their class. This sense of ownership can have significant spin-offs in the management of learning.

■ **Delegate responsibility to students**

In some way this follows on from the point above on making students feel important. Responsibility is one way of achieving this. Passing responsibility to a student for his/her learning should be the key objective of the education process.

■ **Display work**

Whilst this may seem obvious it is not always done. In addition, it is important to change the wall displays and other classroom displays frequently so that fresh work can be displayed. Knowing that they are going to display work can in itself be a motivating factor for many students. This is therefore an integral component in managing learning and can have an influence on the outcome.

■ **Make teaching multi-sensory**

One cannot minimise the challenges faced by teachers in today's classrooms. One of these challenges relates to dealing with the diversity of learning preferences, abilities and cultures. It is important that teaching and learning should be multi-sensory. That means it should be visual, auditory, kinaesthetic and tactile. This involves all the senses and will cater for the range of students' preferences. Many learners with difficulties are often kinaesthetic/tactile learners. That means they learn best by experiencing learning and through hands-on active learning. This is significant as often much of the learning and teaching that takes place in class-rooms is still based on auditory learning just as it was many years ago. It is important to ensure that every lesson and all assessment procedures utilise a range of modalities.

■ **Discover each person's talents and preferences and help them become aware of these**

Just as every football or hockey coach has the responsibility to bring out the best in the individual members of their team then teachers also have a similar responsibility. This means that teachers will need to recognise the strengths in individuals and ensure that students realise that they have these strengths. Students often do not appreciate or even recognise their talents and their strengths. They may compare themselves unfavourably to others and can be unrealistically negative when discussing their own strengths and abilities.

■ **Work with families**

Families can be a significant influence on students. What teachers see in school is only a small part of a much larger picture in students' lives. It is widely recognised that families play an important role in young children's education (Macintyre and McVitty 2004), but this is also the case however in learners further up the school, particularly with adolescent students. Often, but not always, students can have conflicting views with other family members. This can give rise to dissent that may be acutely felt in school. There are many examples of misplaced anger or other emotions which are seen in the classroom but have their roots elsewhere. While it is accepted that there are many significant influences in a student's life, working with families can help to address this. Even if there are no obvious behaviour difficulties it is still important to work with families as much as possible – they can be as source of support for a school and vice versa.

Some examples of how this can be done are shown below for four aspects of school life.

Reading	Behaviour	Learning	Social
Paired reading with carer/parent	Joint home/school reward cards/certificates	Developing metacognitive skills through discussion	Giving an individual a voice – listening to opinions
Shared reading with others in the family	Daily notebook with comments from both home and school	Homework discussion	Group/after-school clubs, sports
Book clubs/ shared magazines	Parent helpers in the classroom	Learning from board games and other game activities	Family holidays, staying with friends

It is important that some thought is given to this aspect to ensure both school and home are in harmony and in communication with each other.

■ **Use positive reinforcement – avoid punishment**

Children of all ages respond better to positive reinforcement. This is because the 'fear' element has been removed and has been replaced by the 'please' element. Children will respond better to all types of situations if they feel a significant adult wants them to do so – and for themselves, not because an adult wishes it. This is also a significant step towards assuming responsibility for their own learning and behaviour.

■ **Always have extension work ready for those who finish before others**

This takes place at the planning stage and it is an important part both of classroom management and of ensuring all learners' needs are met. It is too easy to think up extension work on the spur of the moment when you realise that a student has finished before others. Extension work needs to have a purpose otherwise students can become de-motivated – even those students who are usually keen to learn.

■ **Respect the culture of the individual**

Knowing a student involves knowing about the culture of that student. This is important particularly in relation to accessing and utilising literacy. During a recent trip to schools in the Gambia in Africa I noted that the means of teaching literacy in some schools was through song. Music, dance and movement are very important in African culture and reading and other learning skills can be taught in this way. Similarly with some traveller communities in Europe and elsewhere. Their literacy traditions are very much steeped in oracy and story telling. It is crucial therefore that some knowledge of the cultural preferences of a young person are known, respected and incorporated into planning learning. This will help students to feel respected and will help aid in the management of learning in the classroom.

■ **Develop classroom habits**

Children feel more secure when they know what they are doing and where they are going. A structure and routine can help considerably when working with children on consistency in learning and behaviour. It is also best if the children themselves are involved in developing these routines. 🖭 (See CD Rom Activity 17 – Six steps to good time management.)

Motivation and stimulation

Many of the techniques for classroom management are based on providing motivation and stimulation to ensure students want to learn. Students who want to learn are less likely to provide behavioural challenges than those who are less motivated. Chapter 2 of this book looks at motivation in some detail but basically the main ways of making sure of motivation include:

■ Ensuring the task is related to the student's **interests**.
■ Ensuring the student appreciates the **value** of the task.
■ Ensuring the student can **achieve** the task.
■ Ensure additional **extension** work is available.
■ Ensure that **feedback** is available throughout the task and also immediate feedback at the end.
■ Ensure the student is **emotionally** prepared for the task and is comfortable in the learning environment.

Questioning and responding

Questions can be a means of constructing and managing co-operation in the class and in fact a means of accelerating learning. Some questing techniques can however accelerate classroom **disruption** through confrontation. It is important that the right type of questions is used and in the right way. Some suggestions on good and bad questions are shown below.

Good questions/bad questions – five tips

- Try to make the question a request rather than a command (for example, 'Why do we not do it this way' rather than 'Can you do it this way'?)

- Try to tone down the pitch of your voice – a softer tone can be less threatening than a harsh one.

- Do not provide too many questions at once – one question should be sufficient.

- Do not immediately respond to the answer to a question with another question – make a comment on the answer first.

- Use questions for the right purpose – to find out – and not as a means of controlling behaviour.

Feedback

Three types of feedback

1 Monitoring
Feedback can be a means of monitoring student learning and should provide comment on what has been achieved and what has still to be achieved and whether a student is on the right track.

2 Constructive
This should be seen as a method for motivation. Always begin with a positive comment on what a student has achieved. This may seem obvious to a teacher but may not be so obvious to their students. It is important to state these positive points at the outset. Always end also with a positive comment.

3 Negative
This is when the main purpose of feedback is to assess a student's work. Red ink is often used and the feedback centres on telling a student where they went wrong.

There are cases for all types of feedback to be used but essentially feedback should be seen as a **learning** tool and not an assessing one. If a student is not able to learn from the feedback then it has not been provided in the right way.

Developing independence

Students will have control over their learning, and their behaviour, if they feel they have some independence. It is necessary therefore to provide students with opportunities to take responsibility for their actions in order to achieve independence. Responsibility can lead to independence, so it is important that every opportunity should be made to ensure that students can develop independence.

The role of locus of control in developing responsibility and independence can be a crucial one.

- Internal locus of control means that a student has accepted that he/she has responsibility for the outcome.

- External locus of control means that he/she would shift the responsibility to some external influence.

It is important therefore that students develop an internal locus of control and this will pave the way for accepting responsibility and developing independence.

EXAMPLE – EXTERNAL LOCUS OF CONTROL

I failed my essay because – 'the teacher did not tell us what to do'.

EXAMPLE – INTERNAL LOCUS OF CONTROL

I failed my essay because – 'I did not study the relevant pieces of information'.
Having an internal locus of control is important for behaviour management and self-regulation of behaviour.

Behaviour management

What is bad behaviour?

Exactly what do we mean by bad behaviour? It could be argued that there is no such thing as bad behaviour – perhaps 'inappropriate behaviour' may be a better term. Some inappropriate behaviours are not necessarily bad. Some children have difficulties in judging when a behaviour is appropriate, and when it is not and children with autism/Asperger's syndrome often have this difficulty. Similarly children with ADHD (attention disorders) can have a difficulty in impulse control and can act or say something without first thinking it through. These factors can lead to inappropriate behaviour.

Appropriate behaviour can be developed though social skills programmes. Activities such as turn taking, group discussion and role play can all help in the practice of developing appropriate behaviours. Appropriate behaviour therefore needs be learnt and children need to have opportunities to practise different types of behaviours in different types of situations. Circle Time activities can allow children to undertake sharing activities and also other type of activities can involve making children feel special and worthy through practising complimenting and showing consideration to each other.

Rewards and intrinsic motivation

This is discussed earlier in this book. Behaviours can be modified through rewards but this can only work if a child sees the reward as worthwhile. Ideally what we need to do is to get children to shift to 'intrinsic rewards' and therefore intrinsic motivation. This will take time, and for some children quite a lengthy time. But any reward system should be planned in such as way that the shift from external rewards to intrinsic rewards is the goal of that programme. A reward programme should first identify the different extrinsic rewards such as stickers, points, additional time on favourite activities and so on, and then show how to gradually move to intrinsic rewards such as complimenting oneself and doing a piece of work because they wanted to. Again one of the key aspects of developing intrinsic motivation is the notion of responsibility and developing a sense of responsibility in children.

Responsibility

Rogers (2006) suggests that positive behaviour can emerge from a balance between rights and responsibilities. He suggests teachers need to clarify rights through the use of rules but these rules need to be taught within the context of a supportive classroom environment. He further suggests that the real challenge for teachers is to get students to take responsibility for the consequences of breaking rules. This responsibility should not emerge from a punishment perspective, but from one where students realise that disruptive behaviour affects the rights of others. An example of this is the right to feel safe and that both one's property and oneself are respected. It is this shift from a punishment perspective to the notion of self-responsibility that is crucial in managing learning, effective learning and an effective school.

Classroom control

Classroom control is not about behaviour management but about the management of learning. Classroom control starts at the planning stage and this involves knowing the children as well as planning the lessons and the task. These three factors – children's characteristics, lesson organisation and tasks – are each important in the planning stage. Gathering and reflecting on these can be done at this stage.

Planning – student characteristics

- Learning preferences – visual, auditory, kinaesthetic, tactile.

- Group work/individual work.
- Attention span.
- Persistence – short/longer tasks.
- Responsibility/independence.

Planning task

- Vocabulary.
- Length of sentences.
- Multi-sensory opportunities.
- Pace of work differentiated.
- Learning outcomes varied.
- Worksheet text well spaced with visuals.

Classroom organisation

- Is the layout of the desks helpful in terms of concentration and does it minimise distractions?
- Are the students being encouraged to present their work in a variety of ways including using a word processor?
- Is the lesson broken up to maximise attention?
- Are there opportunities for children to reflect on their learning?
- Is the environment in the classroom as stress free as possible?

Individual Education Plans

The development of an Individual Education Plan indicates that a degree of forward planning has been put in place. The range and nature of IEPs can however vary considerably. Tod and Fairman (2001) suggest that many of the features of effective IEP provision mirror conditions cited as being important for inclusion. They suggest these features include:

- a focus on pupil outcomes;
- provision for diverse needs embedded in whole-school practice;

- the need for formative reflection and analysis rather than merely summative reporting;

- student and parental involvement;

- the use of a variety of instruction;

- rigorous evaluation of the effectiveness of additional or otherwise extra support;

- the sharing of responsibility for children who need support with other adults;

- peer involvement;

- collaborative multi-agency planning.

This list effectively cites good practice which should in fact be adhered to, with or without an IEP. IEPs however do offer a means of checking and monitoring children's progress and can help to provide pointers for classroom management of learning.

Additional and special needs

The term 'special needs' is widely used in most countries. Norwich and Lewis (2007) suggest an interesting distinction between individual, exceptional and common needs. They provide the following:

- Individual needs – arising from characteristics which are unique to the child and different from all others.

- Exceptional needs – arising from characteristics shared by some (visual impairment, high musical ability).

- Common needs – arising from characteristics shared by all (for example, the emotional need to belong and to feel related to others).

When engaging in curriculum and lesson planning it will be necessary to refer to this type of division. It is too easy to misunderstand and mismatch a child's needs. This can be felt particularly acutely in today's climate where there can be a reluctance to use labels to define the nature of needs. This means that teachers need to have an insight into a child's cognitive and attainment profile. 💿 (See CD Rom Activity 13 – Action plan for Special Needs.)

The spectrum of difficulties

The use of labels can be both restrictive and misleading. Weedon and Reid (2005) and Long and Weedon (2006) have attempted to do this for the areas of learning disabilities and behaviour, through an assessment and intervention tool called SNAP (Special Needs Assessment Profile). Rather than profiling labels this tool profiles characteristics – for example in the SNAP there are 19 of these characteristics, including the following:

- working memory difficulties

- information processing

- non-verbal difficulties

- literacy difficulties

- phonological processing

- visual difficulties

- social awareness.

Meeting the needs of all – developing a core of common concerns

As mentioned earlier in this chapter (see page 91), it is then possible to focus on these aspects for a number of children irrespective of whether they have dyslexia, dyspraxia, attention difficulties or are in the autistic spectrum. Their needs may be the same. It is a good idea therefore to identify a core of common concerns and deal with these. For example, some common concerns may be social skills, memory difficulties, recording information through writing and processing speed. These areas can be tackled in a group situation but the needs of children with dyslexia, dyspraxia, ADHD and autism can also still be met using this type of strategy.

Common concerns

Dyslexia	**Autism**
Literacy skills	Literacy skills
Memory	Keeping on task
Organisation	Communication
Keeping on task	Social skills
Communication	Self-esteem
Social skills	Processing speed
Self-esteem	
Processing speed	
Dyspraxia	**ADHD**
Literacy skills	Literacy skills
Memory	Memory
Organisation	Organisation
Keeping on task	Keeping on task
Communication	Communication
Social skills	Social skills
Self-esteem	Self-esteem

(with permission, Fil Came, Learning Works Int) www.learning-works.org.uk

Key Points to Remember

- The successful managing of learning stems from informed planning.
- Pro-active planning is the key to successful classroom management.
- A child's needs and comfort zone are paramount.
- Individual needs should be acknowledged as well as those of the whole class.
- Teaching and learning priorities need to be identified at the planning stage.

Managing Learning

Principles

Observation

Strategies

Proactive

Managing Learning

20 key principles

1. work with student

2. acknowledge all efforts

3. individual feedback

4. cater for all

5. plan

6. anticipate problems

7. learning preferences choice

8. consult

9. remember names

10. student choice/teacher direction

11. student feels important

12. delegate responsibility

13. display work

14. multi-sensory teaching

15. recognise talents

16. work with families

17. positive reinforcement

18. extension work prepared

19. respect individual culture

20. develop classroom routines

The effective school

It is important to develop effective classroom strategies to motivate learners, but strategies can be more effective if schools have a distinct learning ethos. An effective school is one with a learning ethos that is experienced and shared by all students and staff.

This chapter will describe the factors that contribute to an effective school by looking at:

- school climate and school ethos

- the role and development of emotional literacy

- the inclusive policies of a school, including the importance of values and community awareness

- whole-school programmes aimed at developing areas of learning such as thinking skills programmes, social awareness and self-esteem, such as Circle Time activities.

School climate

Having visited hundreds of schools in a professional capacity one of the most striking features is the almost immediate feeling one gets from entering a school and walking along a corridor. These feelings can indicate a welcoming school and provide an indication of its identity and aims. This can stem from wall displays, noise level, the behaviour of children, the friendliness of the 'meet and greet', arrangements for visitors and many other factors that together can provide insights into the climate of a school.

School climate – four types

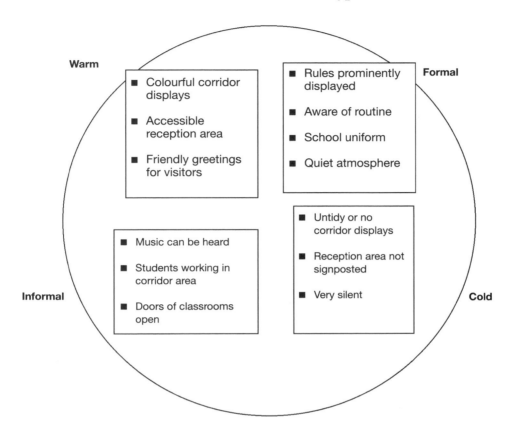

School ethos

The school ethos stems from the school climate and will directly influence students' work ethics and how they conduct themselves both with their peer group and within the larger school community.

Developing a positive school ethos is important as it can influence the following areas:

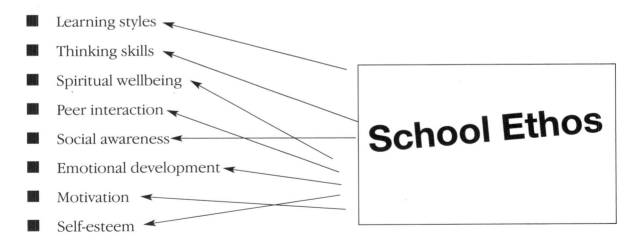

- Learning styles
- Thinking skills
- Spiritual wellbeing
- Peer interaction
- Social awareness
- Emotional development
- Motivation
- Self-esteem

School Ethos

Eleven pointers for a positive school ethos 💿 **(see also CD Rom Activity 14 – School Ethos Checklist)**

■ *Develop a learning rich environment*

This can be done by ensuring all teachers are aware of the role of learning and recognise the importance of developing thinking skills. It is important to differentiate between learning and performance – learning is a process, performance is a product. It is easier to measure performance as this often relates to attainment level and this can be a measure of progress. But some aspects of learning are not so easily measured – and it is only through working with students over a period of time that progress in learning skills can become evident. Students also very often measure their success by results. It is crucial to ensure there is a learning culture in a school as well as a performance one. This can be achieved through projects on learning such as 'How I Learn', 'Learning Styles', 'How to be a Positive Learner'.

■ *Music*

Music can be uplifting and the right kind of music can enhance learning. It can create a positive and stimulating yet tranquil atmosphere in a school. Music in the corridors and in all classrooms can be an indication of a warm and learning-focused school ethos.

■ *Student space*

Students spend a vast part of their day in school – they need to have a feeling of belonging and this can be accomplished more easily if they have their own sense of space. Some children need a safe place to withdraw to and often schools do not have this. If this is not possible there are a number of other ways that can contribute to a sense of belonging. For example, displaying students' work in the corridor; ensuring students are involved in some of the decision-making activities of the school; getting students to show visitors round the school and being involved in some way in parents' evening and other school social occasions.

■ *Prioritise emotional literacy*

Emotional literacy, to have any real impact on the education and lives of children, has to be fully absorbed and fully included in a whole-school ethos. Killick (2006) suggests that an emotionally literate school needs to consider the organisational climate, organisational change, bullying, teacher stress, Circle Time, curricular issues, managing behaviour, communication, motivation, feedback, thinking skills and the development of interpersonal skills. Killick also relates emotional literacy to emotional development and to the development of cognitive learning skills. This emphasises the point that effective learning and emotional wellbeing are intrinsically interconnected.

■ *Celebrate success*

Success can be celebrated through individual achievements but also through whole-school activities. It is important that students see school success and not just individual success as being of importance. This can help students develop a school identity and contribute to the sense of ownership that is so important for a positive school climate. Success can be celebrated through any aspect of school life – it does not have to be a titanic achievement – and it can be something that may be of little significance outside of school.

■ *Stress-proofing a school* 💿 *(see also CD Rom Activity 15)*

There are significant arguments to suggest that stress is a systemic variable which means it can be embedded within a school's system (Reid 1997; Dunham 1995). It is important to recognise that factor and to ensure that stress-proofing a school focuses on the system. At the same time it is also important for individuals to participate in activities that can act as de-stressers such as recreational events, yoga, sports, reading, and so on. Yet whilst these activities can be successful in reduce stress, the good effects can be quickly undone if individuals are working in a system that induces stress. Ideally, to protect staff against undue stress it is important to offer stress-reducing activities but to also ensure the system is as stress free as possible. There are many potential stressors in a school's system and the influence of these on staff needs to be examined and addressed. Factors within the system that can contribute to systemic stress include:

a)   The staff room – this should be as clam and as clutter free as possible and a separate staff work room should be provided.

b)   Paperwork – this is on the increase and its sheer quantity can be quite intolerable for some teachers. It is important that this is recognised and every effort made to reduce this type of workload. Whilst it is acknowledged that record keeping and administration are important, an efficient system will manage to keep administration to a minimum and ensure that it does not impose an intolerable burden on individual teachers.

c)   Access to management – it is important that the lines of communication are obvious and that management is accessible. This might mean that certain times in the school week are allocated to access and consultation with management.

d)   Sharing in the decision making – stress can be increased when an individual feels he /she has no control over decision making. It is important to ensure that staff are consulted and have some influence in decisions – this can help significantly towards the creation of a stress free school system.

■ *Value the individual*

It can be too easy to become absorbed in developing the good reputation of a school and doing things for the good of that school. It is worthwhile however to ensure that individual needs are not overlooked. This applies to both staff and students. Activities such as a dress down day or doing something special one afternoon of the week can be both stress reducing and team building. 💿 (See CD Rom Activity 16 on stress proofing the teacher.)

■ *Value motivation*

McLean (2004) discusses the qualities of a motivated school. He argues that motivation is a school's responsibility and it is quite distinct from developing student self-esteem. The factors surrounding and influencing the learning experience will contribute to student motivation and these factors can be in the school system. Much of this stems from the school ethos, the degree of staff satisfaction and the student incentive to succeed. But before this can be realised schools have to possess and value a learning ethos. Some suggestions for this are made in Chapter 2 (see page 18).

■ *Appreciate difference*

It is important to recognise diversity. This includes cultural diversity as well as individual personality differences. Efforts should be made from a whole-school perspective to ensure school is culturally aware. This can be noted by the use of welcome signs in different languages and acknowledging the festivals and traditions of different cultures.

■ *Collaboration with parents and the whole community*

School should be seen as a community resource and it is important that community links are available and that visitors from the local community are brought into school. Parents should also be involved in this and efforts should be made to ensure that they are made welcome. One way of doing this is to allocate a room for parents which will help them meet each other as well as school staff.

■ *Recognise the needs of staff*

Although school is for students it will only run smoothly if the staff are trained, happy and can work as a team – it is important therefore to recognise the social and professional needs of all staff.

School policies and the effective school

One of the essential factors of an effective school is clarity of roles and clarity on the school position regarding essential elements of learning.

The school handbook for staff can be vital and everyone should be familiar with its contents. School policies on homework, literacy, numeracy, special needs, communicating with parents and discipline can all ease levels of staff uncertainty and ensure role clarity.

The role of management

A great deal of the responsibility for an effective school rests with the school management. It is the school management that determines the ethos and the ethics of their school. An effective school will certainly have effective management.

School management – five signposts for effective school management

1 Democracy

It is important that each member of staff has some influence in the decisions of their school. One of the most stressful factors in any institution is a lack of perceived control (Reid and Hinton 1999). This means that employees must feel they have some influence and control over the work environment, including workload and the roles they play in the institution – and it is notable that role overload and role conflict are two of the most prevalent producers of institutional stress (Reid and Hinton 1999). This feeling can only be achieved if staff have a genuine part to play in the decision-making process and their views are taken into account. The key word here is 'perceived', as often school management may feel they are taking staff views into account but staff may feel differently. The most important factor that can be considered therefore is the ability to listen to the views of staff and to accept their opinions. Otherwise, no matter how democratic management may think a school is, this view will not be shared by staff.

2 Values

School management have to have a set of values that can motivate and support both staff and students. Ideally these values should be shared and the common goals of management, teachers and students should be obvious. It is important to decide on school goals – a school mission statement can often do this and there are some very motivating and stimulating mission statements around. A mission statement can help the different facets of a school to gel and to clearly proclaim the values of that school.

3 Communication

It is important that a management team is able to establish and maintain effective communication links with staff, students and parents. Communication should be a two-way process and the links should be open. This means that specific times should be allocated when management are available for individual consultation and this should be seen as being of high importance.

4 Presence

An effective management is one which has a presence and can be seen to be accessible but it is important that the presence is seen as a positive one. Remote management does not lend itself to collaborative organisation. At the same time the management presence should be seen as purposeful otherwise it may be counter-productive.

5 Culture

It is management's responsibility to ensure that the culture of the local community is reflected in school. All cultures need to be considered in all aspects of school life, such as wall displays, welcome signs in different languages, extra curricular events, parent activities, school meals and accommodation. Visitors can notice very quickly if a school is culturally aware and if it reflects the local community.

Student autonomy

An effective school is one which realises that students need experience in self-advocacy. This can be achieved through giving students practice at determining their own personal study and in some cases choice over timetabling. Student choice can lead to student autonomy and this can allow a student to be a self-advocate. This is training for life and a significant aspect of life training skills. Self-advocacy is important for students to form their own opinions and not to be influenced or intimidated by others.

Social skills programmes can be seen as a means of facilitating practice in self-advocacy. Activities such as decision making, making judgements and forming and justifying opinions can all form an integral part of self-advocacy programmes. An example is shown below.

I think this rule is fair because...

If we did not have this rule ... might happen.

List three things you may want to vote for if you had the chance. Why would you vote in this way?

Key Points to Remember

- Effective learning stems from an effective school.

- The needs of staff are an essential consideration in the development of an effective school.

- A school should be seen to be accessible, culture friendly and student friendly.

- It is important to recognise the values of individuals and to ensure these are acknowledged in the development of clear policies and procedures.

- It is vital to build into the school routine team building and school building activities that can help both staff and students celebrate success.

The Effective School

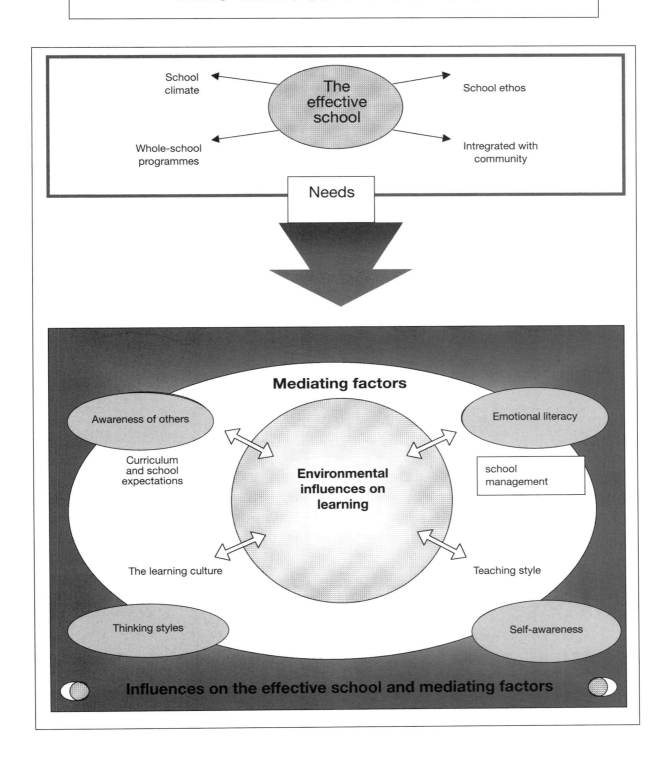

School climate

The effective school

School ethos

Whole-school programmes

Intregrated with community

Needs

Mediating factors

Awareness of others

Emotional literacy

Curriculum and school expectations

Environmental influences on learning

school management

The learning culture

Teaching style

Thinking styles

Self-awareness

Influences on the effective school and mediating factors

Reflection

This chapter will:

- sum up the key points of the book

- provide additional pointers for developing effective learning in an effective school environment

- offer some reflection on the key themes of the book.

 (See also CD Rom Activity 20 – Snapshot for learning.)

★ KEY POINTS

IT IS IMPORTANT TO EMPOWER LEARNERS TO HAVE CONTROL OVER THEIR OWN LEARNING

This is one of the key themes of the book – effective learning is about having control over your learning experience. This means a learner will know the resources to use, know the length of time that can be spent on any one activity, the learning sequence and essentially be able to direct, monitor and assess their own learning.

IT IS IMPORTANT TO ENCOURAGE LEARNER INDEPENDENCE

This can be achieved more readily and more successfully if the whole-school policy and ethos are directed towards that goal. It is too easy for learners to become dependent on a teacher so it is important that learner independence is achieved through learner choice, decision making, learning activities and encouraging students to become aware of their own learning process.

IT IS IMPORTANT TO ENCOURAGE INTRINSIC MOTIVATION

This can help learners decide on their own motives for tackling a learning exercise. This is a whole-school responsibility and needs to be management led. The learning environment and the learning experience must be motivating for learners and this can be achieved through recognition of shared goals and acknowledging learning preferences. It is important to encourage self-evaluation through self-assessment and self-monitoring.

THE TERM 'LEARNING PREFERENCE' MAY BE MORE USEFUL THAN 'LEARNING STYLE'

This indicates that the mode of learning is not fixed and although students may have a preference most can adapt to different types of learning situation. A learning preference is particularly useful when tackling new and challenging learning. It is often best to have learners utilise their learning preference to begin with in order to obtain a better understanding of the area. An additional learning preference implies a more comprehensive meaning, that learning style and preference would include a learning environment and the interaction between a learner and the learning materials.

HOW THE TASK IS DEVELOPED AND PRESENTED HOLDS THE KEY TO EVENTUAL SUCCESS

Learning can be successful or unsuccessful depending on the task. It is important to ensure that the task can be successfully carried out which means that its preparation is important and steps need to be taken to ensure it is effectively differentiated for the student. This includes how the task is presented as well as the learning outcome. Students often fail because the task is beyond them. If this is the case then the onus is on the teacher to differentiate the task and break it down into smaller steps so that learners can succeed. It is crucial that learners can attribute their success as due to their own efforts and not because of support from the teacher. If they attribute success as a result of receiving support they will find it difficult to become independent and autonomous learners. It is important they attribute success to their own efforts and this is why a task must be achievable.

ORGANISATION IS THE KEY TO AN EFFECTIVE MEMORY

This means being able to organise and make information meaningful at the point of learning. Therefore when making notes the students should be able to use appropriate and meaningful headings, sub-headings and recognise how the information can be applied to their practice or their existing schema. They should be generating a conceptual understanding at the point of learning. Often students are preoccupied with obtaining the facts and then try to make sense of these facts afterwards. This is too late as much of the thinking surrounding the initial learning is lost. Students need to obtain the ideas and concepts at the point of learning and later reflect on these from a position of understanding.

EFFORT SHOULD BE MADE TO CONSIDER THE IMPACT OF THE LEARNING ENVIRONMENT

This includes the design of the classroom, the wall displays, lighting and seating arrangements. Music and movement should also be considered – for some learners a silent, static environment is not the most conducive for effective learning.

SELF-DIRECTION AND SELF-MONITORING ARE ESSENTIAL

This is in order for students to take responsibility for their own learning and means that students need to ask questions of themselves as they are learning. They need to know the questions to ask such as: What have I to do here? How does this relate to what I already know? What else do I need to find out? These types of questions provide scope for self-reflection and evidence that the student is beginning to take responsibility for their own learning.

IT IS IMPORTANT TO MAKE EVERY ATTEMPT TO DEVELOP AND ENHANCE SOCIAL LEARNING

For some, learning together can be challenging but it can also provide stimulation and develop thinking and facilitate re-framing and accommodation of the opinions of others. Many learners can work in groups without experiencing these aspects of learning. It is useful therefore to monitor and structure the quality and the processes involved in group work.

KEY TO CLASSROOM MANAGEMENT ARE PLANNING, PREPARATION AND REFLECTION

This provides knowledge of the students, an analysis of the tasks, the purpose of the tasks and the different means of presenting the information. A range of strategies for assessing the performances of the students should also be considered as well as the range of resources needed for tasks. This will ensure that the learning experience is managed which makes classroom control significantly more easy to implement. It allows for students who can be disruptive to be given a task appropriate for them. It is also important to reflect after a lesson on how it could have been improved and why. It is worthwhile to apply the same principles to teaching as one would to learning.

FEEDBACK IS IMPORTANT FOR DEVELOPING LEARNING SKILLS

Time should be allocated to provide feedback not only on the outcome of the task but on the learning process a student went through. It is important to enter into a dialogue with students on how they achieved and responded to tasks. This helps students access metacognitive skills – namely self-knowledge on how they learnt. It also allows the teacher to obtain a picture of students' methods of processing information.

SCHOOL CLIMATE AND SCHOOL ETHOS HAVE MUCH TO OFFER

This is specifically in helping students to become effective learners. Effective learning is not only an individual responsibility, to it is a whole-school responsibility. Effective learning should be integral to the school system and the school ethos can promote success and motivation. It is important that staff in schools recognise this and seek to ensure that school has a positive learning ethos and the school environment is learning-rich. School assembly can be an important part of this, as well as the role of music, classroom and school design, the notion of emotional literacy and the opportunities for success to be celebrated in a whole-school fashion.

VALUE STAFF AS WELL AS LEARNERS

It is important that the school has values and that these values are clear to all. Part of this should however be the need to value staff. Time and effort should be made to stress-proof a school. This is more than promoting the individual means of reducing stress but also requires a look at institutionalised stress and addressing this. It is important to recognise this as a factor that can affect student performance. Effective learning stems from an effective school.

(See CD Rom activity 21 on reflection and Activity 22 and 23 on My Personal Learning Profile.)

Reflection

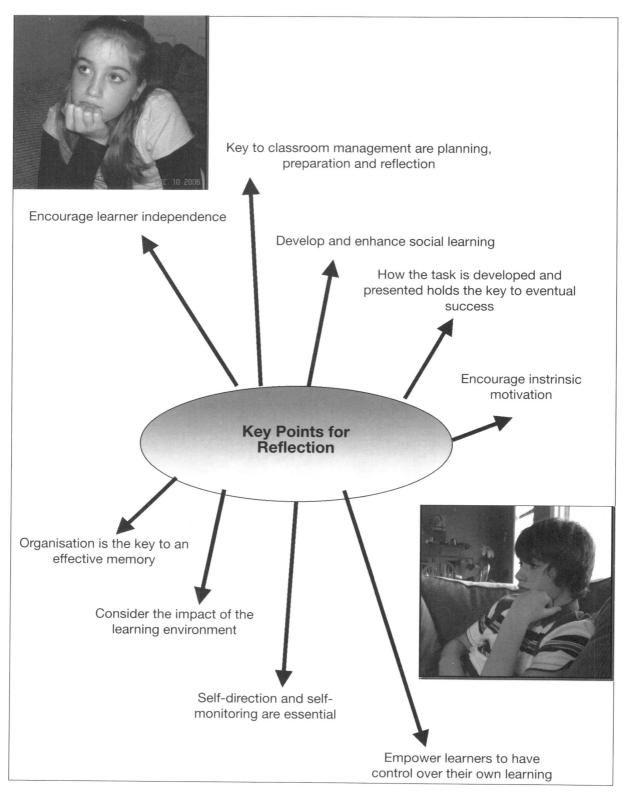

Key to classroom management are planning, preparation and reflection

Encourage learner independence

Develop and enhance social learning

How the task is developed and presented holds the key to eventual success

Encourage instrinsic motivation

Key Points for Reflection

Organisation is the key to an effective memory

Consider the impact of the learning environment

Self-direction and self-monitoring are essential

Empower learners to have control over their own learning

Appendix – Useful Resources

Sources and support

This appendix will:

- focus on the range of supports that can enhance the learning experience and learning skills of students

- inform teachers and professionals on the wide range of materials available to develop classroom learning and teaching.

Sources of information

Resources for support and strategies

The Intelligent School (Second Edition) (2004)
Barbara MacGilchrist, Kate Myers and Jane Reed
Sage Publications, London
This book offers a practical resource to schools to help them become more intelligent organisations. The book draws on a wide range of theoretical and practical positions discussing school effectiveness, learning about learning and teaching for learning. The authors also provide their own nine intelligences framework for school improvement.

Supporting Effective Learning (2002)
Eileen Carnell and Caroline Lodge
Paul Chapman Publishing, London
This book focuses on young people as learners and shows how their learning in school can be supported. One of the purposes of the book is to support the shift from teaching

to learning. The book also discusses the need to learn in context and the value of a learning community. The authors suggest that learners need to learn about learning and teachers have a crucial role in helping to achieve this. The book also looks at 'learning rich' environments and how the school system can support learning at every level.

The Teacher's Toolkit: Raise Classroom Achievement with Strategies for Every Learner (2002)
Paul Ginnis

Crown House Publishing, Carmarthen, Wales (www.crownhouse.co.uk)

This teachers' toolkit contains ideas and game activities for teaching and learning. Section 2 alone contains 50 such game activities. There is also a section of the book on tools for managing group work, behaviour and personal responsibility, as well as suggestions for audit tools to evaluate the impact of different aspects of learning.

Learning Styles and Inclusion (2005)
Gavin Reid

Sage Publications, London

This comprehensive book contains practical suggestions for utilising learning styles within an inclusive context. There are chapters on the learning environment, models of learning styles, learning profiles, teaching and learning, effective learning and inclusion. Contains visual summaries of each chapter and is written in a very accessible manner.

The Power Of Diversity (2004)

Barbara Prashnig, Creative Learning Company, PO Box 106 239, Downtown, Auckland, New Zealand (www.creativelearningcentre.com/products.asp?page =PODBOK)

The author suggests that everyone has a unique style of learning, thinking and working, but very few people consciously learn or work in a way which is best for them. *The Power of Diversity* has been written to help people discover their preferred way of learning and in turn to help them succeed. It is designed as an easy-to-read workbook that introduces the concept of learning styles and explains the important part these styles play in learning. There are also examples from schools and educational institutions around the world.

Failure to Connect: How Computers Affect Our Children's Minds – For Better Or Worse (1998)
Jane Healy

Simon and Schuster, New York

This book that unravels the 'glitz' and 'novelty' of computer technology and the impact it has on learning and on children's health. This is a constructive book that provides sound advice which can help children use technology effectively and provides good advice to parents in particular. Jane Healy explains the difficulties and dangers faced by parents and suggests to them that 'in the case of the child under seven there are few things that can be done better on a computer and many that fail miserably by comparison' (p 218). In this book Dr Healy investigates the effects of computer technology on all possible areas affecting the child – social, cognitive, emotional and personal. Jane Healy is also the author of the popular *Your Child's Growing Mind* (1994) published by Bantam Doubleday, New York.

Get Ahead: *Mind Map Your Way to Success* (fifth edition) (2001)
Vanda North with Tony Buzan
B.C. Books, Dorset

This user-friendly book provides examples of mind maps® and how they can be used in every aspect of learning. There are also clear illustrations on how the brain works and why mind maps® can be effective, particularly in relation to associating, linking and connecting. This book will be particularly useful for those taking up mind mapping for the first time. (Also *Brain Child – How Smart Parents Make Smart Kids* by Tony Buzan (2003) Thorsons Press, London. This book explains how the brain develops and provides a range of simple things that can be done by parents to help a child develop skills in thinking and learning.)

Learning Toolkit Vol 1 and volume 2 (2002)
Fil Came, Gina Cooke and Mel Brough
Learning Works, 9 Barrow Close, Marlborough, Wilts, SN8 2YY
(www.learning-works.org.uk)

This comprehensive two-part toolkit provides a most valuable resource for teachers. It is well organised with stimulating activities neatly presented in logical units. Volume 1 is on personal learning and Volume 2 on learning tools. There is a clear overview and user guide which is also in mind map form that shows the content and purpose of each of the volumes. Volume 1 has activities on personal learning, learning styles, multiple intelligences, emotional literacy and communication skills. Volume 2 contains units on study skills, memory trainers, energisers, thinking skills and team skills. There are also teachers' notes clearly marked in a different colour of paper from the student resources. Together, these result in an excellent resource for teachers.

Ten Best Teaching Practices: How Brain Research, Learning Styles, and Standards Define Teaching Competencies (second edition) (2005)
Donna Walker Tileston
Corwin Press, Thousand Oaks, CA

In this second edition the author provides classroom teachers with a practical guide to motivating teaching practices. An update of the original it details differentiated teaching strategies, such as teaching for long-term memory, collaborative learning, higher-order thinking skills and technology integration. There are also interesting anecdotes illustrating how each teaching practice can be employed in a practical environment, tips on how to encourage students to incorporate self-motivation in their own learning through personal goals and analysis on how the brain absorbs learning.

Strategies to Relieve Stress in the Classroom: A Practical Handbook for Teachers **(2002)**
Geoff Rowe and Fil Came
Learning Works (www.learning-works.org.uk)

This is a very useful, short, but very practical book on stress. It consists of teachers' resources on understanding stress, the vocabulary, signs and symptoms and how our bodies react to stress. There are materials that can be photocopied on techniques for reducing stress.

Behaviour Management – A Whole School Approach **(2001)**
Bill Rogers
Paul Chapman Publishing, London

Excellent and very readable book on behaviour management. Essentially the book promotes a whole-school approach looking at implementing policies and practices that can permeate across the whole school. The theme of the book is positive discipline and developing proactive practices. There are also chapters on supporting colleagues and on developing whole-school policies. The book is very comprehensive and written in a lively style.

The Motivated School **(2003)**
Alan McLean
Paul Chapman Publishing, London

This book is about creating a school that promotes policies on practices on developing motivation. The emphasis is on self-motivation and this is discussed in relation to both the theoretical models of motivation and examples from practice. The author also highlights the features of a motivated school.

Learning styles/ thinking styles models

Six Thinking Hats **(1995)**
Edward De Bono
Little Brown and Co., Boston

This book describes De Bono's view on thinking through the analogy of six thinking hats. The book aims to allow people to, for example, separate emotion from logic and creativity from information. Essentially De Bono defines and describes the nature and contribution of different types of thinking. Different colours are used to describe different types of thinking. For example, a white hat's thinking relates to facts and figures; a red hat to emotions and feelings; a black hat to negative assessment; a yellow hat to speculative and positive thinking; a green hat to creative and lateral thinking and a blue hat to focusing and controlling thinking.

Teaching Elementary Students Through Their Individual Learning Styles (1992)
Rita Dunn and Kenneth Dunn
Allyn and Bacon, Boston, MA
This book describes the use of a well-researched learning styles model – the Dunn and Dunn model – and shows its applicability for students in elementary schools. Chapters include an understanding of learning style and the need for individual diagnosis; identifying students individual learning style characteristics; redesigning the educational environment; global and analytic approaches to teaching and teaching style and; expanding your strengths your way. There is also a chapter on resources for getting started with learning style instruction and appendices showing the extensive research based on the Dunn and Dunn model and the instruments for identifying learning or teaching styles.

Teaching Secondary Students Through Their Individual Learning Styles (1993)
Rita Dunn and Kenneth Dunn
Allyn and Bacon, Boston, MA
This book follows the same format as the one above but focuses on secondary students. The appendix also provides references and research based on this model.

Teaching to the Brain's Natural Learning System (2002)
Barbara K. Given
ASCD (Association for Supervision and Curriculum Development), Alexandria, Virginia, USA
This book focuses on the five major learning systems identified by Given, bridging neuroscience with educational frameworks. There are chapters on each of the five systems – emotional, social, cognitive, physical and reflective. Given also relates the framework to other learning style models such as the Dunn and Dunn model and Gardner's multiple intelligences. The book also discusses the educational implications of each of the learning systems.

Inside Styles – Beyond the Basics: Questions and Answers on Style (1996)
Anthony Gregorc
Gregorc Assoc. Inc., 15 Double Day Road, Box 351, Columbia, CT 06237-0351 (www.gregorc.com/)
This book provides answers to some key questions on learning styles, such as definitions and models. It illustrates how the Gregorc model differs from other established models. The book discusses the therapeutic value of styles, ethics and morality, teaching and administrative styles and sources and resources.

Relating with Style (1997)
Diane F. Gregorc
Gregorc Assoc. Inc., 15 Double Day Road, Box 351, Columbia, CT 06237-0351
This book uses the Gregorc style delineator and explores human relationships from concrete and abstract sequential and concrete and abstract random styles. It provides insights into thinking patterns, attitudes and beliefs, feelings and emotions, from the perspectives contained in the Gregorc model.

The Dominance Factor – How Knowing Your Dominant Eye, Ear, Brain, Hand and Foot Can Improve Your Learning (1997)
Carla Hannaford
Great Ocean Publishers, 1823 North Lincoln Street, Arlington, Virginia 22207-3746
In this book Hannaford, inspired by Dennison's work on educational kinesiology, describes her assessment system called Dominance Profiles. The book explains what is meant by a Dominance Profile and provides a key to the 32 Dominance Profiles from the different combinations of hand, eye, ear and foot dominance. The author then goes on to show how dominance profiles can impact on human relationships and education. The book gives an insight into the use of dominance profiles.

Smart Moves – Why Learning Is Not All In Your Head (1995)
Carla Hannaford
Great Ocean Publishers Inc., 1823 North Lincoln Street, Arlingon, Virginia 22207-2746
This text shows how the body is involved in learning from infancy to adulthood. The book is divided into three parts – Part 1 looks at the role of the body in emotional and intellectual processing; Part 2 presents a special emphasis on brain gym activities to activate full brain functioning; and Part 3 on nurturing and protecting our learning systems discusses various factors that create learning difficulties.

Experiential Learning (1984)
David Kolb
Prentice-Hall, Englewood Cliffs, NJ 07332
This scholarly work describes an analysis the nature and impact of experiential learning. The author refers to the roots of experiential learning from the legacy of Denney in higher education, Lewin in organisational development and Piaget from the cognitive development tradition. There are also sections on the process of experiential learning, the structure of learning and knowledge and learning development. This text would be extremely helpful to those engaged in an academic study of the area.

Experiential Learning Theory Bibliography 1971–2001
A. Kolb and D.A. Kolb McBer and Co., Boston, MA
The Learning Style Inventory: Technical Manual (1976)
David Kolb
McBer and Co., Boston, MA
The Learning Style Inventory is a statistically reliable and valid, 12-item assessment tool based on Experiential Learning Theory. It identifies preferred learning styles, and explores the opportunities different styles present for:

- Problem solving
- Working in teams

- Resolving conflict

- Communicating at work

- Communicating at home

- Considering a career.

The Four Learning Styles it covers are:

- Diverging: combines preferences for *experiencing* and *reflecting*

- Assimilating: combines preferences for *reflecting* and *thinking*

- Converging: combines preferences for *thinking* and *doing*

- Accomodating: combines preferences for *doing* and *experiencing*.

The manual features suggestions for understanding, which are:

- The learning cycle; the impact of learning styles on team work; conflict resolution; communication and career choices.

The LSI manual also provides:

- Practical advice for developing weaker styles and through the use of four colours it reinforces learning concepts.

- The instrument is based on a norm population of 6,997 LSI users.

The 4 Mat System – Teaching to Learning Styles With Right/Left Mode Techniques (1987)
Bernice McCarthy
Excel Inc., 200 West Station Street, Barrington, IL 60010
This book provides a comprehensive guide to the 4 mat learning styles approach. The book is in four parts: Learning Styles; Right and Left Brain Processing; The Complete Model and Sample Lessons. A very user-friendly text with detailed and illustrated explanations.

Multiple intelligence

Outsmart Yourself! 16 Proven Strategies For Becoming Smarter Than You Think You Are (2004)
David Lazear
David Lazear Products (www.davidlazear.com)
This book focuses on the theory of multiple intelligences proposed by Harvard psychologist Dr Howard Gardner. This research suggests that each of us possesses at least eight distinct areas of intelligence – eight ways in which we know what we know in our lives,

eight ways we acquire knowledge and at least eight ways we learn and understand. In this book, Lazear views intelligence as a biological, neurological, psychological, sensory reality which occurs throughout our entire brain, mind, body system, and even beyond ourselves in our sociopolitical environment as well. The book presents a comparisions of IQ ('intelligence quotient') and MI ('multiple intelligences') and a personal inventory helps readers assess their own 'intelligence profile', showing those areas of multiple intelligences which are more or less developed. The book also focuses on the use of multiple intelligence strategies to accelerate and deepen understanding and presents 101 activities to awaken full intelligence. Also included is a set of exercises for enhancing and strengthening those intelligence areas which may be under-developed and/or under-utilised.

Multiple Intelligence Approaches to Assessment: Solving the Assessment Conundrum (2004)
David Lazear
Crown House Publishing, 6 Trowbridge Drive, Suite 5, Bethel, CT06801
Based on Howard Gardner's model of Multiple Intelligences, this book provides more than 1,000 specific ideas designed to help teachers accurately assess children's academic progress. It covers the subject areas of Maths, English, History, Geography, Science, and practical and fine arts and also gives practical prescriptive ideas on how to teach to varying intelligence strengths.

Multiple Intelligences in the Classroom (2004)
T. Armstrong
Association for Supervision and Curriculum Development, Alexandria, VA
This updated practical guide for educators incorporates new research from Gardner and others. This new edition includes information on the eighth intelligence (the naturalist), a chapter on a possible ninth intelligence (the existentialist), and updated information and resources throughout the text to help educators at all levels apply MI theory to curriculum development, lesson planning, assessment, special education, cognitive skills, educational technology, career development, educational policy, and more. The book also includes practical tips, strategies and examples from schools.

Myers Briggs Type Indicator – People Types and Tiger Stripes (1993)
Gordon Lawrence
http://www.myersbriggs.org/
Center for Applications of Psychological Type, Gainesville, Florida
This publication provides an interpretation of the Myers-Briggs indicator to help understand different people types, motivation and learning styles. The author also illustrates in some detail how the Myers-Briggs can be used in planning teaching, adapting the curriculum and to understand organisations.

Psychometrics: How To Use Geometric Psychology to Influence People (1989)
Susan Dellinger
Prentice-Hall, Englewood Cliffs, NJ 07332
In this book the author explains how to use geometric shapes such as a box, rectangle triangle, circle and squiggle to accurately reflect one's personality and style of learning. There is reference as to how different personality types respond to different types of situations at home, in the workplace and in social situations (see also Chapter 7).

School Learning and Cognitive Style (2002)
Richard Riding
David Fulton Publishers, London
This book provides an overview of cognitive styles of learning. The author describes cognitive style as 'an individual's approach to organising and representing information' (p 23). The book discusses the nature of cognitive style and relates this to classroom performances and learning preferences. The author also discusses memory and behaviour management.

Cognitive Style and Learning Strategies (1998)
Richard Riding and Stephen Rayner
David Fulton Publishers, London
This book provides an in-depth analysis of cognitive style and the implications for learning style and learning strategies. There are chapters on cognitive style, individual differences, learning and problem behaviour.

Thinking Styles (1997)
Robert Sternberg
Cambridge University Press
This well-known text discusses the nature of thinking skills and why we need them. Sternberg goes on to describe and provide a rationale for his thinking styles model – the legislative, executive and judicial styles. There is also a section on how thinking styles can be applied to schools both in assessment and in teaching.

Differentiation Through Learning Styles and Memory (2003)
Marilee Springer
Corwin Press
The author suggests that traditional instruction and 'paper and pencil' assessment are no longer sufficient for meeting the needs of increasingly diverse student populations. This book therefore provides educators with a guide for differentiation. It includes differentiation by design and differentiation through learning styles and the section on memory provides an overview of how the brain processes, stores, and retains information and how teachers can guide students in accessing this information by utilising their individual learning styles and strengths. The book also includes activities for helping students discover the best ways to retrieve information, for example through mind mapping, debating, role playing, mnemonics, metaphors, rhymes, songs and repetition.

Music

The Mozart Effect (1997)
D. Campbell
Avon Books, NY (www.accelerated-learning.co.uk)

Learn With the Classics – Using Music to Study Smart at Any Age (1997)
Ole Anderson, Marcy Marsh, Dr. Arthur Harvey
LIND Institute, PO box 14487, San Francisco, CA 94114 (www.lind-institute.com and also available from the Accelerated Learning Centre at www.accelerated-learning.co.uk)

An overview of web links

Hemispheric Dominance
Link – www.mtsu.edu/~studskl/hd/learn.html
Dr Carolyn Hopper (2003) *Practicing College Study Skills: Strategies for Success* **(3rd edition), Houghton Mifflin, Boston, MA**
Hopper indicates that as well as linear and holistic, sequential and random, logical and intuitive, verbal and non-verbal, the differences in the hemispheres can also been noted in symbolic *vs* concrete processing. This implies that the left brain can easily process symbols. Symbols such as letters, words, and mathematical notations are important on most educational environments. The left-brained person is usually comfortable with linguistic and mathematical exercises. Left-brained students are able to memorise vocabulary words or math formulas.

Hopper suggests that the right brain, on the other hand, needs information to be concrete. The right-brained person wants to see, feel, or touch the real object. Right-brained students may have trouble learning to read using phonics. They prefer to see words in context and also to see how the formula works. To use the right brain, hands-on activities need to be developed.

Kolb's Experiential Learning Style Model
Link – www.infed.org/biblio/b-explrn.htm

Personality – the Myers Briggs Type Indicator
Link – www.myersbriggs.org/
The Myers Briggs is extremely well used and validated. It has four main indices and from that sixteen types can be derived. The indices are:

- *Extraversion-Introversion (EI)* The EI index is designed to reflect whether a person is an extravert or an introvert in the sense intended by Jung. Extraverts are oriented primarily towards the outer world; thus they tend to focus their perception and judgement on people and objects. Introverts are oriented primarily toward the inner world; thus they tend to focus their perception and judgement upon concepts and ideas.

- *Sensing-Intuition (SN)* The SN index is designed to reflect a person's preference between two opposite ways of perceiving; one may rely primarily upon the process of sensing (S), which reports observable facts or happenings, or one may rely upon the less obvious process of intuition (N), which reports meanings, relationships and/or possibilities that have been worked out beyond the reach of the conscious mind.

- *Thinking-Feeling (TF)* The TF index is designed to reflect a person's preference between two contrasting ways of judgement. A person may rely primarily through thinking (T) to decide impersonally on the basis of logical consequences, or a person may rely primarily on feelings (F) to decide primarily on the basis of personal or social values.

- *Judgement-Perception (JP)* The JP index is designed to describe the process a person uses primarily in dealing with the outer world, that is, with the extraverted part of life. A person who prefers judgement (J) has reported a preference for using a judgement process (either thinking or feeling) for dealing with the outer world. A person who prefers perception (P) has reported a preference for using a perceptive process (either S or N) for dealing with the outer world.

The sixteen types

According to theory, by definition, one pole of each of the four preferences is preferred over the other pole for each of the sixteen MBTI® Instrument types. The preferences on each index are independent of preferences for the other three indices, so that the four indices yield 16 possible combinations called 'types', denoted by the four letters of the preferences (e.g., ESTJ, INFP). The theory postulates specific dynamic relationships between the preferences. For each type, one process is the leading or dominant process and a second process serves as an auxiliary. See the following website for more details on this (www.capt.org/the_mbti_instrument/Overview.cfm).

Multiple intelligence
Links:

- The Multiple Intelligence Inventory (surfaquarium.com/MI/inventory.htm)

- Using Multiple Intelligences (4teachers.org/projectbased/intell.shtml)

- www.creativelearningcentre.com/

Also worthwhile is the University of Minnesota Duluth webpage on learning and learning styles Theory into Practice (TIP) database. TIP is a tool intended to make learning and instructional theory more accessible to educators. The database contains brief summaries of 50 major theories of learning and instruction. These theories can also be accessed by learning domains and concepts. (tip.psychology.org/index.html).

■ www.med.harvard.edu/AANLIB/

Contains an atlas of the whole brain

■ www.braingym.org

Information about Brain Gym©

■ www.circle-time.co.uk

The main site for Circle Time (Jenny Mosley)

Fun Track Learning Centre, Perth, Western Australia,
Mandy Appleyard, Educational Consultant
Unit 2, 590 Stirling Highway, Mosman Park WA 6012
PO Box 134 Mosman Park WA 6912
www.funtrack.com.au

CCET, Centre for Child Evaluation and Teaching, Kuwait.
PO Box 5453, Safat 13055, Kuwait.
www.ccetkuwait.org Centre of Excellence with programmes in English and Arabic,
strong focus on motivation and learning, also have a national helpline for parents and
professionals

www.creativelearningcentre.com
Creative Learning Company, New Zealand

www.mindroom.org
Mindroom – organisation for learning difficulties including ADHD

www.doctorg.org
Loretta Giorcelli's website – highly recommended international consultant

www.alcenter.com
Accelerated learning site

Red Rose School, 28–30 North Promenade
St Anne's on Sea, Lancashire, England, UK
FY8 2NQ
www.redroseschool.co.uk
Have implemented a learning styles approach in the design of the classrooms and in the
delivery of the curriculum.

REACH O-G Learning Center, 850 West 15th St. North Vancouver, BC, Canada
www.reachlearningcenter.com
REACH Orton-Gillingham Learning Center is an academic learning centre that was
formed to assist individuals who are struggling to learn to read or spell. Using the

Orton-Gillingham approach to overcoming language-based learning difficulties, the staff have all been specifically trained to teach reading, writing and basic language skills to students who have difficulties acquiring these skills.

www.teachnet.org
Teachers Network is a nationwide US, non-profit education organisation that identifies and connects innovative teachers exemplifying professionalism and creativity within public school systems. Over 40,000 public school teachers have been involved in the work of Teachers Network in the areas of curriculum, leadership, policy and new media.

www.dana.org
Dana.org serves as a gateway to brain information, provides information about the brain and current brain research, and has a link to validated sites related to more than 25 brain disorders. One link, Brainy Kids Online, offers children, parents, and teachers a site with activities for younger children, puzzles, links to excellent educational resources and lesson plan suggestions.

www.accelerated-learning.co.uk
The Accelerated Learning Centre was formed by The Anglo American Book Company to promote a comprehensive selection of books on accelerated learning.
Provides a comprehensive catalogue of resources for teachers, parents and those in educational management.

www.learning-solutions.co.uk/brain-gym.php
Learning Solutions offers a range of services to schools, individuals and trained providers of The Listening Program®. They are representatives for the UK and Ireland Advanced Brain Technologies, Utah, USA, who are developers of The Listening Program® and other cognitive training tools. The services are offered by Alan Heath author of *Beating Dyslexia – A Natural Way* which contains detailed powerful and effective spelling and memory strategies.

www.learning-works.org.uk
Internationally aclaimed teaching and learning organisation led by Fil Came – range of resources and training courses.
info@learning-works.org.uk

Sage Publications (incorporating Paul Chapman Publishing, Lucky Duck Publishing and Corwin Press)
www.sagepub.co.uk
www.paulchapmanpublishing.co.uk
This publisher provides up-to-the-minute thinking from 'educational visionaries'. Deals with all aspects of education, from initial training to the role of headteachers and consultants. Paul Chapman authors include Bill Rogers, Tina Bruce, Barbara Maines and David Sousa. The book *Learning Styles and Inclusion* by Gavin Reid is published by Paul Chapman which has links with Lucky Duck Publishing and Corwin Press and is a Sage Publications company (www.sagepublications.com).

References

Bruner, J. S. (1965) *The Process of Education*. Cambridge. MA: Harvard University Press.

Donaldson, M. (1978) *Children's Minds*. Glasgow: Fontana/Collins.

Dunham, J. (1995) *Developing Effective School Management*. London: Routledge.

Given, B. K. (2002) *Teaching to the Brain's Natural Learning System*. Alexandria, VA: ASCD.

Killick, S. (2006) *Emotional Literacy – At the Heart of the School Ethos*. London: Paul Chapman.

Kolb, D. A. (1984) *Experimental Learning*. Englewood Cliffs, NJ: Prentice-Hall.

Long, R. and Weedon, C. (2006) *Special Needs Assessment Profile (SNAP B) Behaviour*. London: Hodder Murray.

Macintyre, C. and McVitty, K. (2004) *Movement and Learning in the Early Years: Supporting Dyspraxia and Other Difficulties*. London: Paul Chapman.

McLean, A. (2004) *The Motivated School*. London: Sage.

Piaget, J. (1954) *The Construction of Reality in the Child*. New York: Basic.

Piaget, J. (1970) *The Science of Education and the Psychology of the Child*. New York: Viking.

Reid, G. (2004) 'Dyslexia', in A. Lewis and B. Norwich (eds), *Special Teaching for Children*. Maidenhead: OU Press. pp 138–50.

Reid, G. (2005) *Learning Styles and Inclusion*. London: Sage.

Reid, G. and Hinton, J. (1999 [1996]). 'Supporting the System – Dyslexia and Teacher Stress', in G. Reid (ed.), *Dimensions of Dyslexia: Volume 2: Literacy, Language and Learning*. Edinburgh: Moray House.

Reid, G. (2007) *Dyslexia* (2nd edition). London: Continuum.

Reid, G. and Green, S. (2007) *100 Ideas for Supporting Students with Dyslexia*. London: Continuum.

Tod, J. and Fairman, A. (2001) 'Individualised Learning in a Group Setting', in L. Peer and G. Reid (eds), *Dyslexia-Successful Inclusion in the Secondary School*. London: David Fulton.

Vygotsky, L. S. (1986[1962]) *Thought and Language*. Cambridge, MA: MIT Press.

Vygotsky, L. S. (1978) *Mind in Society: The Development of Higher Psychological Processes*. Cambridge, MA: Harvard University Press.

Weedon, C. and Reid, G. (2005) *Special Needs Assessment Profile (SNAP) Version 2*. London: Hodder Murray.

Index

Page numbers prefixed with A denote appendix entries.